HOW TO ARRANGE
DRIED FLORALS
IF YOU THINK YOU CAN'T

The publisher and designer wish to thank the following companies for providing materials used in this publication:

❀ **Adhesive Technologies, Inc.** for low temperature Craft and Floral Pro™ Glue gun and sticks
❀ **American Oak Preserving Co.** for dried and preserved floral materials
❀ **Beyond the Garden Gate, Inc.** for freeze dried roses and snapdragons
❀ **C.M. Offray & Son, Inc.** for ribbon
❀ **Chartpak** for True Expressions™ rub-on letters
❀ **Crisa Corp.** for glass vases
❀ **DMD industries** for stationery and memory album
❀ **Delta** for Ceramcoat® acrylic paints
❀ **Duncan Enterprises, Inc.** for Aleene's tacky craft glue
❀ **Frontier Imports** for baskets
❀ **Hot Off The Press, Inc.** for the Paper Pizazz™ paper
❀ **Knud Nielson** for dried and preserved floral materials
❀ **Lion Ribbon Co., Inc.** for ribbon
❀ **Luzon Imports** for all TWIGS™ vine wreaths and the birdhouse
❀ **Naturals by Webster** for preserved floral materials
❀ **Nature's Pressed** for pressed flowers
❀ **Schusters Of Texas, Inc.** for dried and preserved floral materials and raffia
❀ **Vaban Gille** for cornhusk wreath and ribbon
❀ **Verdissimo** for preserved floral materials
❀ **Walnut Hollow** for wood picture frame, clock and footstool
❀ **Wang's International, Inc.** for pine wreath, birdhouse lamp and tin watering can
❀ **Winward Silks** for silk flowers

About the Designer:

Anne-Marie Spencer lives in Oregon with her best friend, Laurence, and is the in-house floral designer for Hot Off The Press. Her background includes creating floral designs for many national catalogs as well as traveling abroad to design basketware. Hot Off The Press is happy to have Anne-Marie on our team and delighted to share her talents with you. As you might guess, Anne-Marie is already hard at work on more floral books.

To Paulette Jarvey and Teresa Nelson for all their encouragement, support and great ideas. Please know how much you are appreciated.

Production Credits:

Project editors: Tara Choate, Mary Margaret Hite
Technical editor: Terry Dolney
Photographer: Kevin Laubacher
Graphic designers: Sally Clarke, Jacie Pete, Susan Shea
Digital imagers: Victoria Gleason, Larry Seith
Editors: Teresa Nelson, Lynda Hill, Tom Muir

published by  **LEISURE ARTS® CRAFT LEAFLETS**

P.O. Box 55595
Little Rock, Arkansas 72215

produced by **HOT OFF THE PRESS** INC.

Hardcover ISBN 1-57486-080-1
Softcover ISBN 1-57486-079-8

Canby, OR 97013

HOW TO ARRANGE
DRIED FLORALS
IF YOU THINK YOU CAN'T

Table of Contents

Getting Started

Winning Wreaths

Wall Decor with Elegance & Style

Center of Attention

A flair with the Natural

Dressed and Pretty

Floral Accents & Embellishments

DECK THE HALLS

All About Dried Materials

Dried flowers have been popular since ancient times, used to perfume rooms and personal effects, as well as express emotions and thoughts through the individual meaning of each particular blossom. A rose saved and dried from a loved one's bouquet, was said to endear that person to your heart for all time. Egyptians placed sweet smelling rushes on the floors of their entry rooms to ward off evil spirits; small bouquets and nosegays of flowers were carried by seventeenth century Europeans to ward off the plague.

This old-fashioned tussie-mussie uses many materials readily available because of modern preserving techniques.

This project utilizes dried materials to decorate the vase and potpourri to scent the room.

In the Victorian era, collectors of plant materials pressed, preserved and catalogued their findings and shared them with the world. Enthusiasts soon copied their works, pressing and drying flowers to make arrangements and decorative ornamentation for their homes. Once again dried materials are gaining popularity, fueled by their availability and variety as well as new preserving and drying techniques. No longer limited to a few available everlastings, most of the flowers from the garden can now be found dried or preserved. And because of their lasting quality, they are wonderful alternatives to fresh flowers.

The vibrant roses in this wreath are a recent addition to the materials available through preserving.

Dried Floral Terms to Know

The term "dried florals" encompasses many materials which have been preserved through several different methods.

All the materials in this Wheat Sheaf are air-dried.

Dried: This describes materials that have been air-dried or dried with a dessicant like silica gel. The resulting material is dry and can be brittle. Stems of dried material will snap when bent. Dried materials are commonly field-grown flowers such as larkspur, roses and "everlastings". Dried greenery is recognizable by a light or basil green appearance and brittleness. Many dried greens such as bay leaf and salal are quite popular because of the smooth texture they add to floral designs.

Preserved: These floral materials are easily recognizable by the soft leaves and blossoms. The stems are supple and bend without breaking. Preserved flowers are nearly always systemically dyed in the preserving process and traces of the dye can be seen if the stem is split open. Preserved materials are easy to work with as they do not shatter easily.

Freeze Dried: Freeze drying is a commercial process which involves the removal of moisture from an object through deep freezing and results in fresh-looking flowers; however, they are fragile and can shatter if handled roughly. Most freeze-dried flowers have been treated with a polymer coating after drying to help control breakage. Flowers and fruits are the most common items found in a freeze-dried form. However, freeze-dried loaves of bread and whole vegetables can make wonderful accents.

The freeze-dried snapdragons add a fresh-picked feeling to this design.

The preserved plumosus in this wreath lends a "fresh" quality to the design.

Dehydrated: This process is most commonly used for fruit and vegetable slices. They can be purchased in craft stores or dehydrated at home using a food dehydrator. Purchased materials should never be consumed as they are often coated with polymers as an added preservative.

Pressed: These flowers are characterized by their one-dimensional appearance and are used in flat designs on pictures, boxes, lampshades and book covers. As with dehydrated materials, they can be purchased in craft stores or pressed at home.

Growing & Drying Flowers Today

At one time the best resource for dried flowers was at a local farm, where selections and quantities were greatly limited. Today's demand for quality dried flowers has risen dramatically, and the commercial growing and production of these materials has expanded to meet this rising demand.

There are literally thousands of acres worldwide that are dedicated to the commercial growing, drying and distribution of dried flowers. A large percentage of the dried flowers purchased in stores today are grown in Holland, where fields of flowers can be found spread out for miles in a dazzling quilt of bright colors. In addition, many exotic pods and flowers come from Australia and Africa. Commercial farms often employ collectors who scout the world looking for new products to introduce.

The new varieties are stunning and attention is given to every detail from planting to environmentally safe packaging. Techniques used by these commercial farms have been honed to a scientific precision. Flowers are picked at their peak stage for drying, carefully hung in climate controlled environments where a strong warm airflow current circulates between the carefully spaced bunches, allowing them to dry in anywhere from one to two days.

What this quick drying means to the consumer is superior quality, both in texture and color brightness. Mosses are cleaned and fumigated to be rendered dry, clean and "bug free". Preserved flowers are processed in enormous vats of precisely dyed glycerin and timed for a perfectly preserved product that is virtually identical in color to previous and future batches.

Photos courtesy of Regenboog Dried Flowers.

When it comes time to harvest, people are recruited from all over to work these commercial farms, cutting and sorting the flowers into bunches for drying. Thousand of bunches are handled daily. Another crew will check the flowers for quality after the drying process, then sort them into appropriate sized bunches for resale. Finally, the bunches will be packaged and boxed for shipment all over the world.

Air drying is the simplest and most common method of drying flowers. Depending on the type of material, the bunches can be hung upside down, dried upright in a vase or laid flat.

Hanging bunches is the most common method and will generally provide excellent results. Gravity will pull the materials downward and straight as they are drying. Before hanging, be sure the flowers are dry and remove the lowest leaves to prevent decay. Tie several stems together, separating the flower heads. Be sure to tie tightly; the stems will shrink as they dry, causing loosely bound bouquets to fall apart. Suspend the bunch upside down in a dry, dark room. Check periodically, examining the stem near the flower head for firmness and making sure the blossom is completely dry. Air humidity will determine how quickly the flowers dry. Flowers like roses appear dry on the outside, but may still retain moisture near the center of the blossom.

After wiring the flower stems together, use another piece of wire to hang them well out of reach.

Drying materials upright in a container should only be used with lighter materials. Tall grasses (like pampas) as well as many grains, seed heads and flowers with smaller blossoms, such as hydrangeas and gypsophila, dry well standing upright in a vase because these materials will not droop. However, top-heavy flowers, such as roses, do not dry satisfactorily standing upright because the stem will bend with the weight of the blossom.

Though hanging is the most common method of drying materials, many materials should be dried flat or in a vase, depending on their finished look.

Leaves, cones, mosses, twigs and many grasses can be dried flat. Lay the material on an absorbent surface such as cardboard or newspaper and space the material carefully, allowing air to circulate around each piece. Leaves on stems will retain their natural shape on the stem when dried this way.

How to Color Dried Florals

Spray-painting is the simplest method of coloring dried florals. There are spray paints made especially for this purpose; they are very effective and come in a wide variety of colors. Be sure to use them in a well-ventilated area and protect surrounding surfaces. Begin with a very light misting of paint, holding the flower 6"–8" from the nozzle. Do not spray heavily as the paint will run or the flower will become an unnatural color. If the color is not dark enough, repeat the process, again spraying lightly. Floral paints are available in opaque shades for solid coloring and translucent styles to provide slight tinting to materials. Wood tones, metallics and glitter paints are available for special effects, as well as black- and whitewashes for darkening or lightening a color without changing the tone.

How to Preserve with Dessicants

Dessicants such as silica gel, borax, alum and sand can be used to absorb the moisture from plant material. Silica gel is the best option; it is faster and can be used again. If fine grade crystals are not available, grind the coarser grains with a mortar and pestle; large crystals will bruise the petals of delicate blossoms.

Put a layer of crystals in a container that can be sealed. Lay flowers on top, then layer more silica gel over them, using a small paintbrush to fill the crevices until the flowers are completely covered. Close the container and put it on a shelf. Check the material every two days by gently removing a blossom with a slotted spoon. If it is not dry, bury it again. Remove the blossoms as soon as the petals are dry and brush off any silica gel with a fine paintbrush. The silica gel crystals can be dried out in a warm oven and stored in an airtight container for reuse.

Silica gel can be used over and over again to preserved a variety of flowers and plants.

If you choose to use another dessicant such as borax or alum, it should be mixed with a fine dry sand. Mix three parts chemical to two parts sand. Layer the flowers in the mixture as with the silica gel and follow the same procedures, but wait at least 10 days before checking them.

Some flowers and most leaves can be preserved using glycerine which leaves the material supple; however, the flowers and leaves will change color, often to a tan shade, unless dye coloring is used in the mixture. Glycerine preserved flowers must be colored in the preserving process—they will not absorb the paints. If you are unsure as to the shade or intensity of dye to use, experiment with a few stems first.Mix equal parts of glycerine and near boiling water.

Remove any lower leaves and cut the stem at an angle. Pound the lower stems of woody plants with a hammer to encourage better absorption. Place the stems in a jar with 4" of the solution; single leaves can be soaked in a bowl. Place in a cool, dark room for 6-10 days, checking occasionally. When small beads of glycerine form on the upper ends of the plants, enough has been absorbed. Remove the plant and wash it in soapy water, then pat dry.

Glycerine is absorbed through the stems of materials, making it very easy to use.

How to Press Flowers

An age-old method of drying flowers is to press them. A flower press provides the best results, although pressing between the pages of a book will work. If the latter method is used, press the materials between sheets of parchment or waxed paper to avoid discoloring the book pages. Cut the materials on a dry day and press immediately. Three-dimensional flowers such as roses and carnations do not press well because their shape distorts, but individual petals can be pressed successfully. It is best to avoid plants with fleshy leaves since the leaves are too moisture-dense to press well. To enhance a pressed flower's color, brush colored dry tempera chalk, found in most art supply stores, can be brushed onto the petals of a fresh flower before pressing. After the flower has dried, brush off the excess chalk with a soft paintbrush. Pressing time for all flowers will depend on the petal density, but check after 10 days, then gently remove the flower from the press.

Some techniques for pressing flowers have not changed much through the years.

A microwave oven cuts the drying time to minutes. Because the length of time needed by conventional methods will cause white flowers to discolor, a microwave oven is ideal. Press the flowers between parchment, using microwave-safe glass as a weight. Microwave at ¾ power for a minute at a time until the flower is dry.

Working With Dried Materials

Dried material that is brittle or has been bundled tightly together can be misted with water from a spray bottle to soften it. If the material is still tightly bunched, remove the rubber band from the stems and lightly mist the upper portion while separating the stems. Do not soak the material as it will become soggy and difficult to use. Material will remain soft long enough to use in your project. This is helpful for dried leaves when using them to make a wreath.

Misting a tightly bound bundle of materials can make them easier to work with.

The blossom size of dried flowers with layers of petals such as roses and peonies can be made larger by holding the blossom over hot steam, then gently teasing the petals open with a small, firm paintbrush. Repeat the process

until the blossom is opened to your satisfaction. Do not force the petals as they can tear or separate from the blossom. Potpourri oil can be added to the steam to infuse the blossom with a delicate fragrance.

Steaming a flower head allows you to push the blossom open to create a bigger-looking flower.

To prevent shedding of petals, spray the finished arrangement with a light coat of sealer. There are products made especially for this purpose and can be found in craft stores.

When working with wreaths, creating a design perimeter is important. When the design is hung on the wall, it should extend around the sides to nearly touch the wall. A grapevine wreath base should not be visible from a side view unless the vines are intended to be a visible element of the design.

Creating a design perimeter ensures a pretty wreath when viewed from all sides.

To keep finished projects clean, use a blow dryer on a cool setting once a week to keep the dust away. If dust accumulates, use a commercial product for cleaning dried flowers. Be sure to read the instructions carefully, as some products can stain ribbon. If in doubt, cover the ribbon before use.

To avoid breakage, the larkspur is among the last things added to this tall design.

When making a tall arrangement with many stems inserted closely together, save the most brittle elements until last, especially when freeze-dried stems are included in the design. This helps avoid breakage caused by brushing stems with your hand when inserting materials.

If making an arrangement, remember that the stem ends of dried flowers are generally unattractive. If using a clear vase and no floral foam, fill the vase with moss or something decorative that complements the planned arrangement. Marbles, pebbles and potpourri are attractive vase fillers and will help hold the stems in place. If using foam, cut the foam smaller than the vase opening, leaving a ½"–1" space between the sides of the vase and the foam. This allows decorative materials such as potpourri or moss to be slipped between the vase and the foam to conceal the foam.

Potpourri conceals the foam in this glass vase.

Dried flowers hate water and humidity. Do not display dried designs outside as they can mildew; however, they will become brittle if hung close to a heat source. Keep arrangements out of high traffic areas where they may be bumped. To prevent fading, do not display them in direct sunlight.

Repairs and Storing

Although dried flowers are more fragile than silks, a broken flower head or two is no reason to discard an arrangement. A broken head can be floral taped to a new wire stem (see page 28) and inserted back into the arrangement. If an arrangement starts to look old or worn, inspect it carefully before throwing it out. Many times an old or worn-looking arrangement can be revitalized by removing one or two materials and replacing them with new. In European countries, dried flowers are an important decorative element and there are businesses whose sole focus is the repair and rejuvenation of dried arrangements. If you can construct it, you can modify it!

Carefully storing dried materials not only makes them last longer, but makes them easy to use.

Repairing a blossoms is easy and can keep a project looking beautiful.

If stored well, dried materials have a relatively long shelf life. For longer term storage, flowers should be stored loosely in packing boxes. Wrap each bunch in tissue and lay them in rows in the box, alternating the direction of the tops of the bunches in the rows. Do not mix preserved and dried flowers in the same box as the moisture in the preserved materials will cause the dried materials to decay. For short term storage, bunches can be hung upside-down from a clothesline in a dry room. All florals must be completely dry and stored in a dry environment as moisture will cause deterioration.

Mixing Dried & Silk Floral Materials

Many times, silk flowers can substitute for, or add to, dried flowers in a design. While dried materials add texture and natural colors to arrangements, this can be achieved with silk substitutions as well. They can also add effects that are not possible with drieds. For example, vinyl pine and Christmas greenery make a great base to embellish with dried flowers, such as the Majestic Metallic Wreath on page 137. They are available in garlands and centerpieces, inexpensive and can add richness to holiday decor.

Silk flowers also have the advantage of bendable stems and greenery, allowing them to be angled or curved in dramatic ways. Peaches & Cream on page 48 features stems of silk heather that have been curved. Although they are not the focus of the design, they add texture to the composition and enhance the lines. Silk baby's breath is available in many colors and can replace dried or preserved

Add dried materials and seasonal accents to an artifical pine wreath for a fast, easy and wonderful holiday decoration.

Shiny latex berries are used on this wreath to contrast the dried materials.

baby's breath. The stems can be easily bent and angled to fill the open spaces in a design.

To expand the look of nature's bounty in a design, latex berries, fruits, pods and vegetables are available in a wide variety of colors, textures and styles. The Forest Wreath on page 109 features latex berries to complement the natural pods and grasses and add rich colors.

The varying sizes of silk blossoms provide alternatives for creating focal points. Using dried flowers in floral designs can be challenging as the sizes are generally less than 1" wide. The Willow Eucalyptus arch on page 66 features three silk roses which provide the balance for the elegant draping of the eucalyptus on each side of the arch. In this case, dried florals might get lost among the other elements of the design. Silks can provide the focus while dried flowers accent them, adding a natural look to the design. Silk materials provide versatility while enhancing the colors and textures.

Substituting Florals

A vast choice of colors and types of dried and preserved flowers makes it simple to substitute materials and tailor a design to match a certain decor. If the colors are to be changed, first determine the dominant color in the design and buy the same amount of the similar-sized flowers listed in the desired color. Repeat through the list, substituting your chosen colors for the ones listed. When you've gathered all the flowers, hold them together to make sure you like the way the new colors blend or contrast with each other.

If one flower in a design is unavailable in your store, look at the material in the photo or the identification section on pages 6–15 and try to find one that is similar to it. Check to make sure it is approximately the same size and that there is as much foliage as needed. If the substituted flower is smaller that the one listed, more may be needed to fill the design; if the substitution material is larger, less may be necessary to complete the design.

Substituting materials in dried wreaths and arrangements is as simple as choosing elements with similar characteristics.

Fillers such as rice grass, baby's breath, bloom broom and caspia can easily substitute for each other. They have similar characteristics—fine flowers or seeds which extend equally well among the larger components of the arrangement.

If the design calls for focal blossoms such as dried dahlias and they are not available, try preserved carnations, roses or daisies. All are about the same size in diameter and will have the same impact when used as a focal point. Ti tree can be substituted for leptospermum, stirlingia, heather or even larkspur; all are line flowers in the arrangement.

Substituting cones or mosses when the correct type cannot be found is as easy as replacing it with a pod or cone of a similar size and color. If several styles of pods are needed to complete a project, it's important that different pods are used, if those exact ones can't be found. If all the same ones are used, the design may become boring; different styles add texture and interest to a piece. When substituting mosses, again, look for a similar color and texture. For instance, sphagnum, mood and shag moss can substitute for each another.

Protea flats could be substituted for the lotus pods in this arrangement.

achillia

amaranthus

amaranthus,
hanging

ambrosinia

ammobium

dahlia blossoms

Dried,
Pressed

dudinea

basil

heather

alyssum

daisy

fantasia

four
o'clock

avens

ivy

bridal wreath

golden
asters

honeysuckle

bluebell

cockscomb

bougainvilla

cosmos

desert
marigold

Indian
paintbrush

larkspur

chrysanthemums

christina
grass

caspia

button
flowers

baby's breath

barley

avena

baby everlastings

mini baby's breath

bear grass

& Preserved Flowers

brisa maxima

shooting star

verbena

poppy leaves

viola

maidenhair fern

maple leaf

Queen Anne's lace

rabbit's foot fern

tamarac

lupine

lobelia

salvia

sweet clover

bloom broom

plumosus fern

brisa media

bromus grass

bromus secalinus

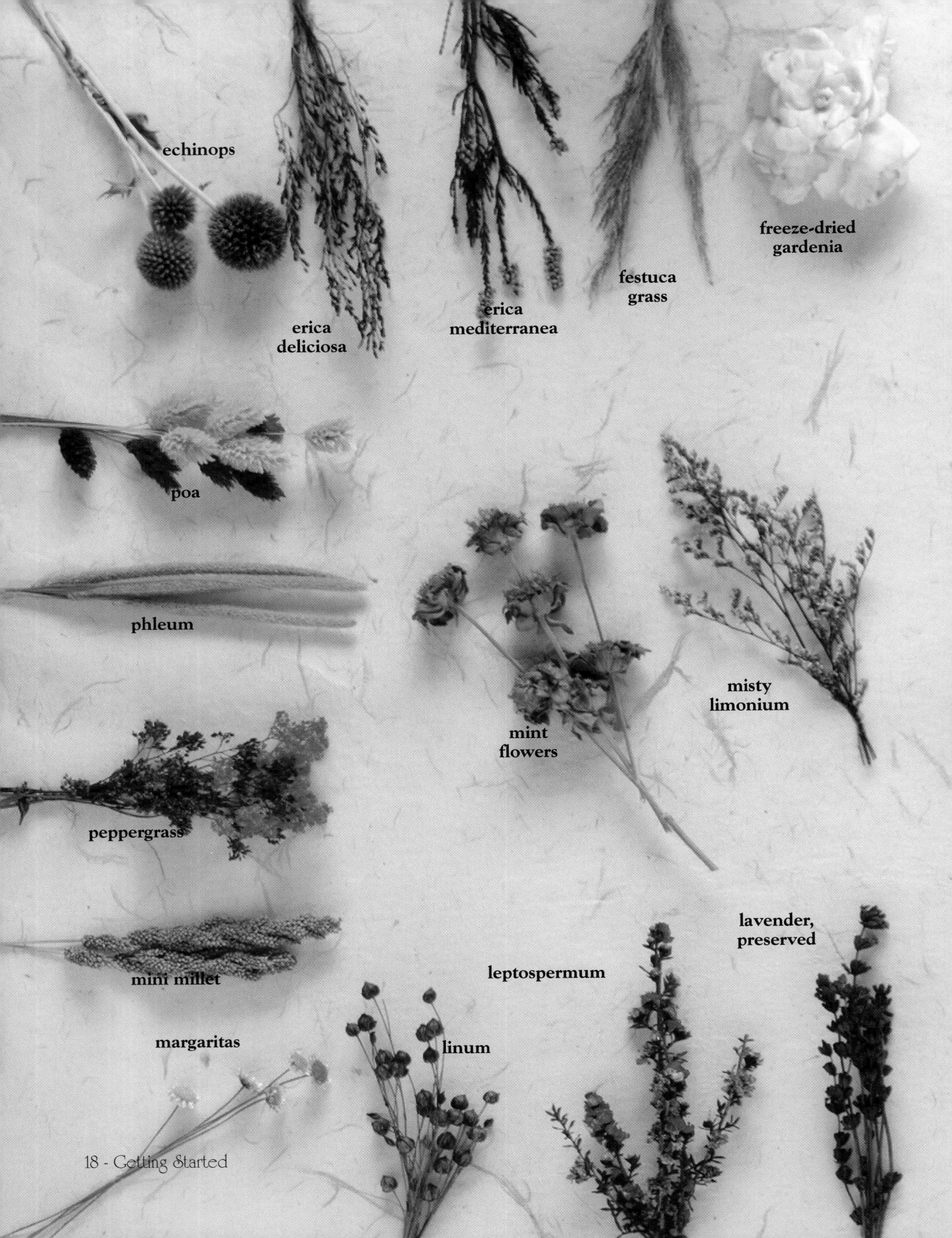

echinops

erica deliciosa

erica mediterranea

festuca grass

freeze-dried gardenia

poa

phleum

misty limonium

mint flowers

peppergrass

mini millet

lavender, preserved

leptospermum

margaritas

linum

genista

German statice

heather

hill flowers

hydrangea, preserved

pennyroyal

oregano

hydrangea, dried

isolepsis grass

lavender, dried

larkspur

lagurus

ixodia daisies

rice flower

rice grass

rhodanthe

ti tree

sweet Annie

wild oats

suworowii statice

wheat

tulyp star

sunflower (dried)

starflowers

solidago

stirlingia

strawflowers

roses, dried

rose, freeze dried

rose,
preserved

roses

rose, preserved

wheat,
black-bearded

yarrow

safflower

wheat,
club

setaria

Siberian
statice

snapdragon

silene grass

sinuata statice

bay

austral fern

bracken fern

cedar

boxwood

running cedar

Leaves,

princess pine

salal, preserved

plumosus fern

salal, dried

needle grass

oak, transparent

pepperberry foliage

oak, Italian

hops

eucalyptus,
spiral

eucalyptus,
willow

Fraser
fir

holly

ivy

Ferns & Greenery

leatherleaf
fern

lecchio

sprengeri fern

tree fern

lepidium

magnolia
leaves

mahonia

myrtle

mini
holly

ming
fern

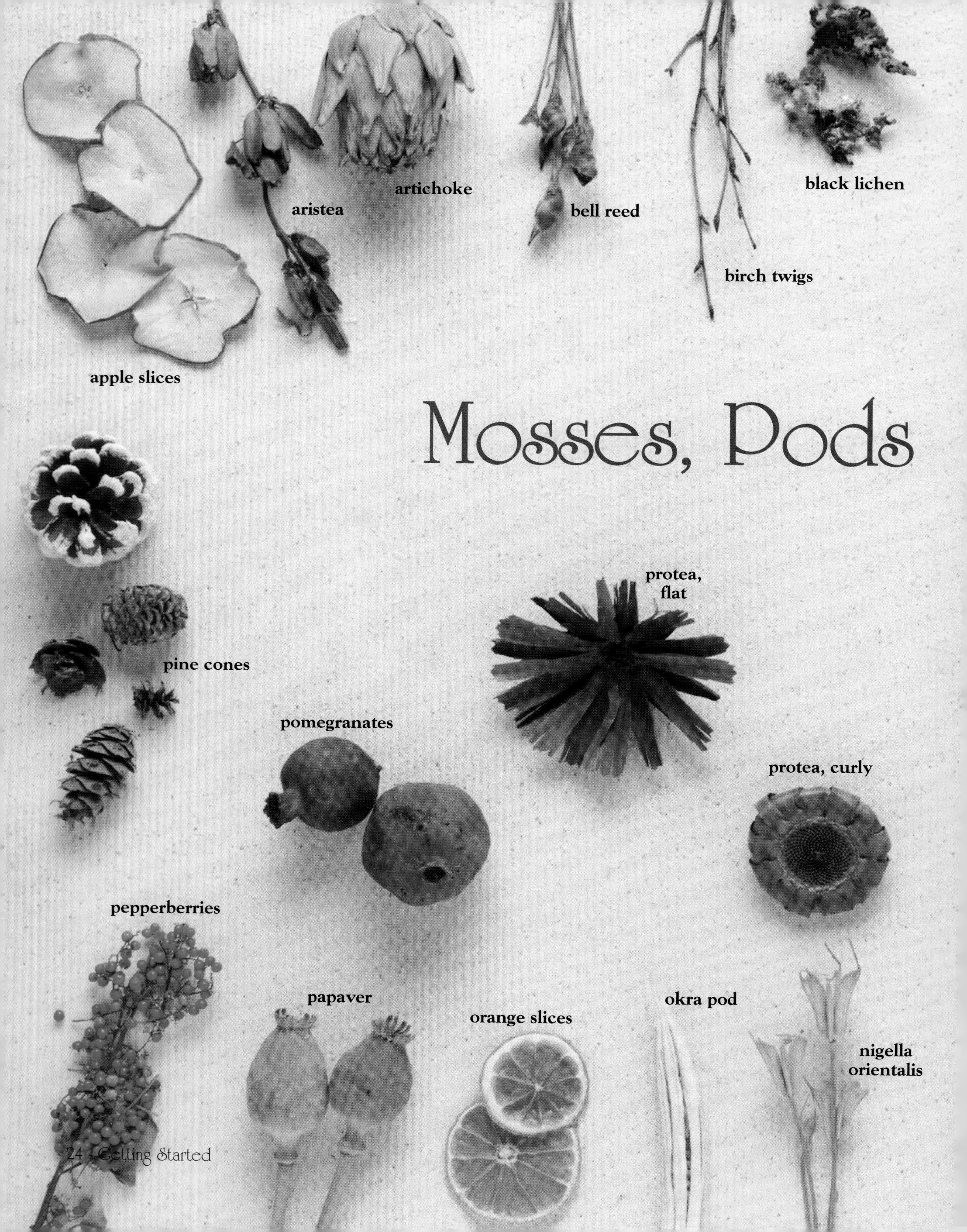

apple slices

aristea

artichoke

bell reed

black lichen

birch twigs

Mosses, Pods

pine cones

protea,
flat

pomegranates

protea, curly

pepperberries

papaver

orange slices

okra pod

nigella
orientalis

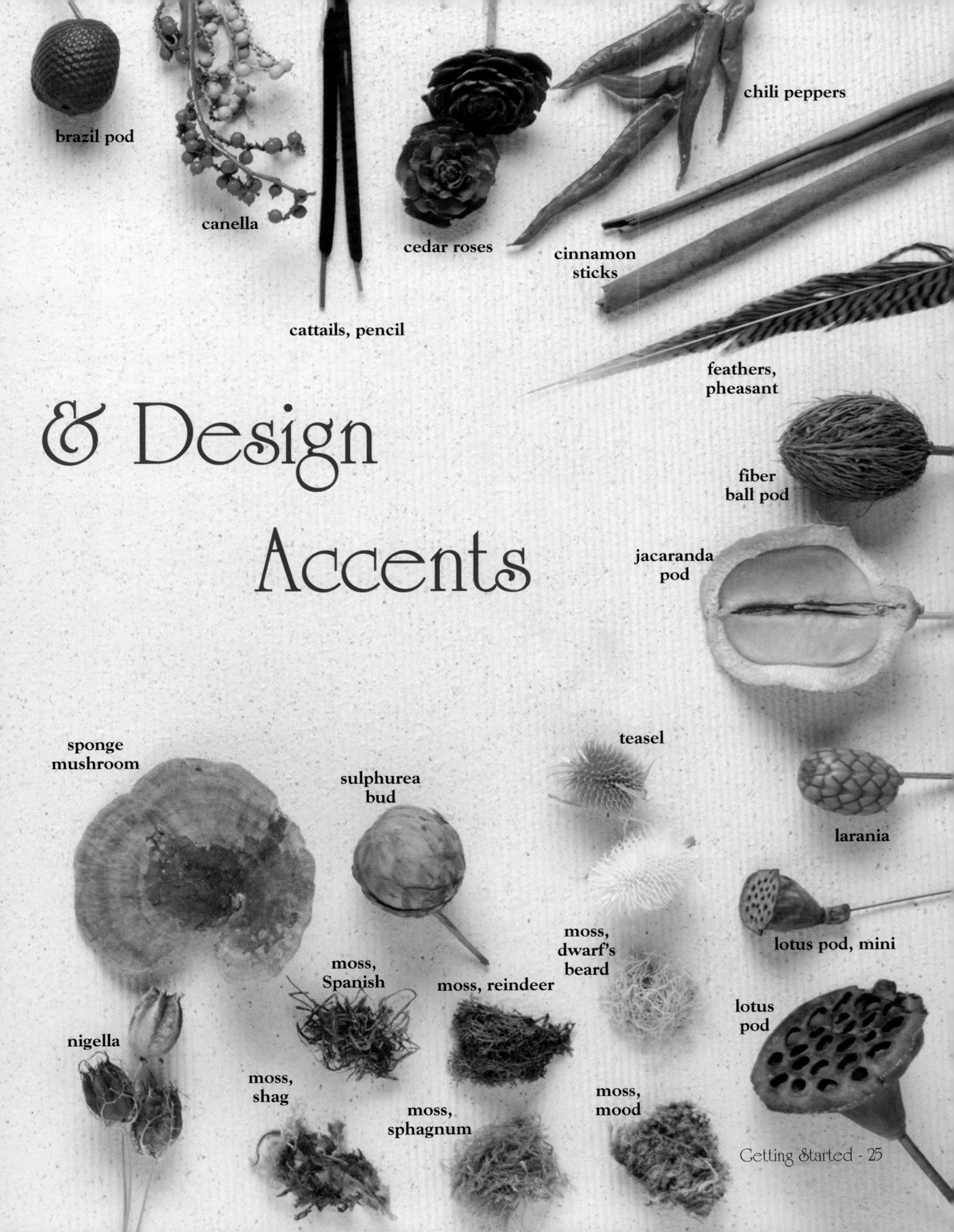

brazil pod

canella

cattails, pencil

cedar roses

chili peppers

cinnamon sticks

feathers, pheasant

& Design

Accents

fiber ball pod

jacaranda pod

teasel

sponge mushroom

sulphurea bud

larania

moss, dwarf's beard

moss, Spanish

moss, reindeer

lotus pod, mini

nigella

moss, shag

lotus pod

moss, sphagnum

moss, mood

Tools, Supplies & Putting It All Together

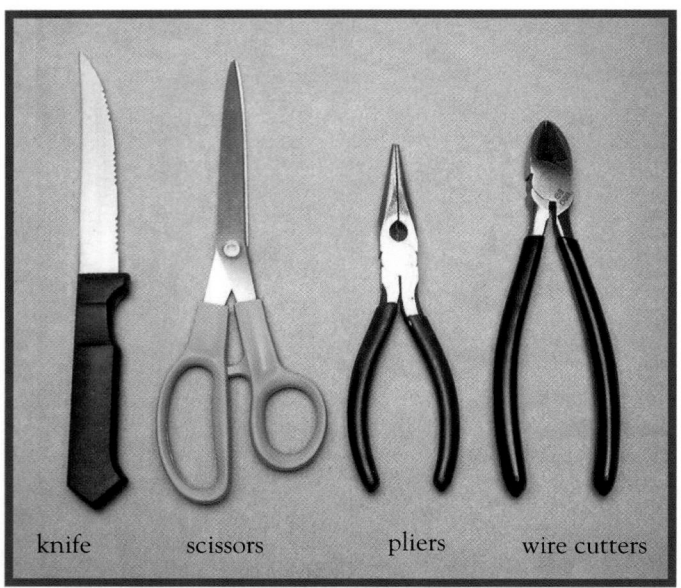

knife   scissors   pliers   wire cutters

The following pages include explanations and photos of all kinds of floral tools and supplies. Sometimes it's difficult to know just which supplies are really needed to complete a project; this information should eliminate some of the confusion and make it easier to decide what is needed and when. Included are some tips for using certain supplies, too.

Tools

A sharp serrated knife, scissors, needle-nose pliers, and heavy-duty wire cutters are valuable tools in floral work. The wire cutters need to be sturdy enough to cut through the heavy stems. Use the pliers to twist wires together, saving tender hands and fingernails. The knife is used to trim floral foam to fit a base. Scissors should be sharp enough to cut ribbons, and shouldn't be used to cut wire, which will nick and dull the blades.

Wires

(A) Wires are measured by gauge—the smaller the number, the heavier the wire. 18–20 gauge wire is used to lengthen or strengthen flower stems (see "Floral Tape," page 28). 22–24 gauge wire is a nice weight for bows or loop hangers. 30-gauge wire is very fine and can be used to attach stems to bases and to secure ribbon loops. **(B)** Paddle wire is fine-to medium-weight wire rolled onto a wooden paddle and is used whenever a continuous length is needed.

(C) Cloth-covered wires come in either green or white. Green wires resemble flower stems and blend in well with designs. The white wire is useful when doing bridal work. Both are available in stem weight as well as lighter weights for securing items together.

(D) Chenille stems can be used instead of wire to secure bows. Because of their fuzziness, they don't slip as easily—and because of their wide range of colors, they can be matched to the ribbon.

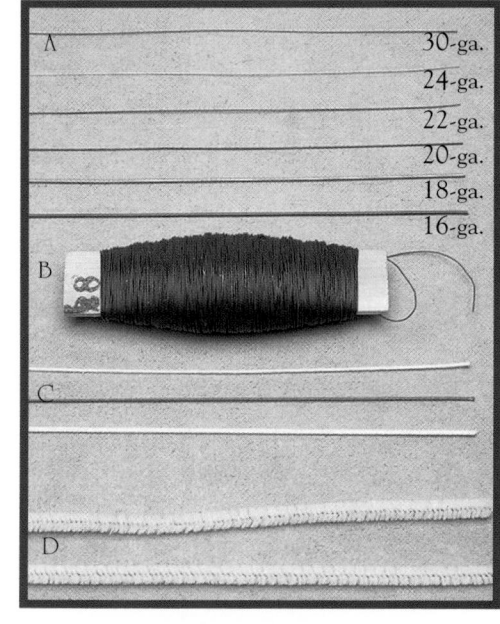

A   30-ga.
24-ga.
22-ga.
20-ga.
18-ga.
16-ga.

B

C

D

Making Wire Loop and U-Pin Hangers

First decide the best placement for a hanger so the project hangs correctly (some projects, such as a garland, will require more than one hanger). Insert a 6"–10" length of 24-gauge wire into the back of the base (or among the vines of a wreath). Bring the end back out and twist both ends together, forming a loop. If the object is solid and a wire can't be inserted, make a wire loop first and hot glue it to the back.

An easy hanger for a straw or foam wreath can be made by bending the ends of a U-shaped floral pin back and inserting them into the wreath. For extra strength, secure the U-pin with hot glue.

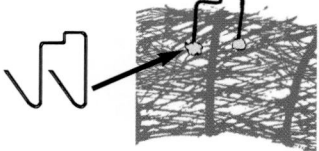

Glues

Tacky craft glue effectively secures stems in floral foam. Dip the cut stem into glue, then insert it into the project. Gluing keeps stems from twisting in or dislodging from the foam, ruining established design lines.

Hot or low temperature glue guns are handy for floral designing. The low temperature gun is safer, but not as secure as hot glue when used on items preserved with glycerine. Apply glue to the stem end, then insert it into foam or onto the base. Hold the item for a moment until the glue sets. Glue sticks are available in different formulas; make sure you use the correct stick for the job and the gun.

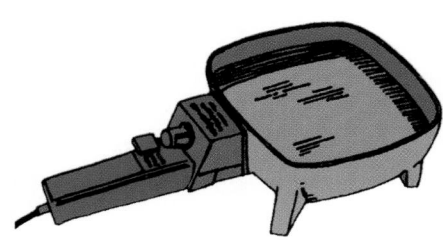

Glue pans, which hold a pool of melted glue at a constant temperature, are useful when you have a lot of gluing to do, since they let you keep one hand free by allowing you to dip the stems.

Floral Foam

Floral foam is available in two types: fresh or "wet" foam and dry foam. Wet foam should be used only for fresh flowers. Because it is made to soak up water and hold it for the fresh stems, it's too soft for dried and silk arrangements. Dry foam, designed to be used with silk and dried flowers, is firmer and holds stems more securely.

To prepare dry foam prior to attaching it to a base, use a serrated knife to cut it to size—trim away as much as possible, leaving a smaller area to be concealed. If the foam is to fit into a wreath, be sure to trim away enough so the foam fits snugly against the inner side.

Use the knife to round the top edges and corners of the foam. This will make it easier to cover with moss or excelsior and make the "ground" where the stems are inserted look more natural. Do not cut away so much of the foam that it no longer extends the correct amount above the rim of the container. It's much easier to achieve a natural,

growing look in an arrangement if you're able to insert stems into the foam sides to extend parallel with the table. Usually no more than 1" needs to extend above the rim to achieve this effect.

To attach floral foam to a base, glue or wire it in place. To wire it, first cover an area on the top of the foam with a strip of moss or excelsior, then wrap a 30-gauge wire length over the foam and around the base, twisting the ends at the back to secure. The moss prevents the wire from pulling through the foam.

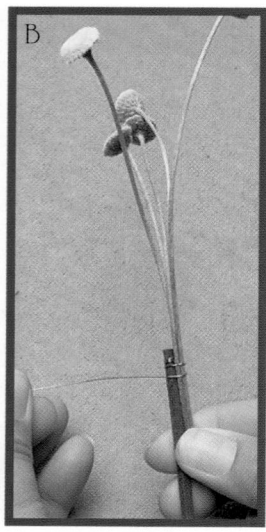

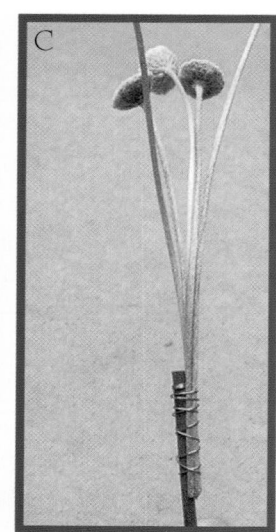

Wood Picks

These add length or strength to floral items. To add a wired wood pick to a cluster of dried flowers:

(A) Position the flowers in the cluster at varying heights, then cut the stems in the same place.

(B) Place the stems against the pick; wrap the wire around both the pick and the stems.

(C) Continue wrapping down the pick for 1", then wrap back up the stems, using all the wire.

Wood picks also come without wires. These can be floral-taped to stems or glued to the backs of stem-less items such as pods, charms and novelties.

U-Shaped Floral Pins

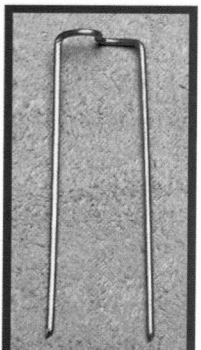

Also called "greening pins," these are used to pin moss, ribbon loops, or other items into foam. If the item being secured has a tendency to cause the pen to spring out of the foam, apply a dab of glue to the pin ends before inserting.

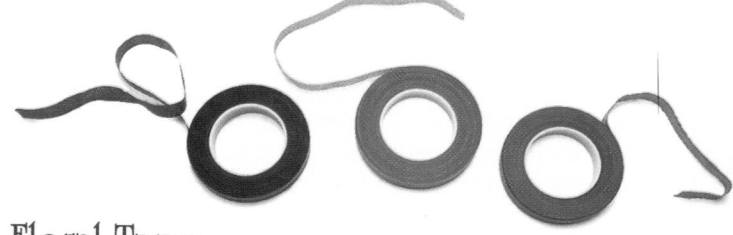

Floral Tape

This is a paper tape which has a waxy coating; stretching the tape as it's being wrapped makes it stick to itself. Use floral tape to secure wire or a pick to a flower stem, lengthening or reinforcing it (also called "stemming a flower").

(A) Place a length of 18-gauge wire next to the stem of a flower.

(B) Wrap the stem and the wire together with floral tape, gently stretching the tape so it adheres to itself. Tape to the end of the wire.

Measuring & Cutting Floral Stems

A "stem" refers to the entire stem of flowers as purchased. When cut apart, the pieces are called "sprigs" or "branches."

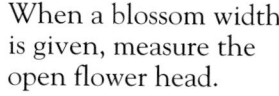

When a blossom width is given, measure the open flower head.

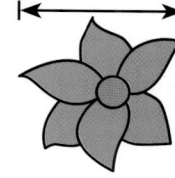

When a blossom height is given, measure only the blossom.

When a stem length is given, measure only the stem.

When a flower length is given, measure from the top of the blossom to the end of the stem.

Unless otherwise specified, flower measurements given within a project include 1½"–2" of stem to be inserted into the design. By cutting the stems with extra length, you are able to adjust the height of the flower within the arrangement, playing with it until it's exactly right. Using tacky craft glue to secure stems lets you, while the glue is still wet, pull out a stem that is too long, trim, reglue and reinsert it without destroying the foam. If a stem is too short, lengthen it with a stem wire (see "Floral Tape," page 28), then cut to the correct length.

Wiring a Cone

To wire a cone to attach it to a base:

(A) Use a 10" length of 24-gauge wire. Measure 3" from one end and insert the wire between two rows of cone petals near the bottom.

(B) Wrap the wire around the cone, pulling tightly, then twist the wire ends so they extend from the cone. Use these wire ends to attach the cone to the project. For another look, wrap the wire among the upper petals so the bottom of the cone will show in the project.

Three Ways to Attach a Pick or Stem to a Pod or Cone

(A) Drill a hole into the bottom. Fill the hole with glue and insert the blunt end of an unwired wood pick into the hole.

(B) Wrap the wire of a wood pick around the cone petals, pulling it down inside the cone. Wrap all the wire completely around the cone and then around the pick.

(C) Hot glue a U-shaped floral pin to the cone bottom.

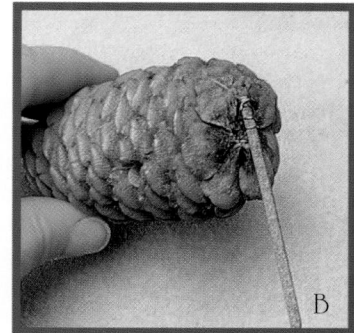

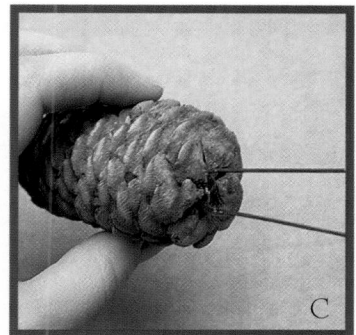

Ribbons & Bows

Some people think one of the most difficult tasks in making a floral project is making the bow. Not so! The easiest way to learn is to buy a reel of inexpensive acetate ribbon—enough so you don't feel guilty using as much as you want—and practice making bows. The freedom of knowing you can use as much as you want until you get it mastered makes learning much easier than if you use the expensive tapestry ribbon you bought just for a certain project. Eventually, making bows will become second nature.

We've included instructions, photos and illustrations of the bows used in this book. Generally, if choosing a narrower ribbon than the one suggested, more will be needed. More loops will also be necessary to make sure the bow has the same impact within the design. Likewise, if a wider ribbon is chosen, you'll probably want fewer loops to make sure the bow doesn't overpower the project.

Ribbons and bows are beautiful additions to florals, but the styles of ribbons available are almost endless, and it can be confusing to choose just the right pattern for a project. However, you'll find that the flower colors and the style of the arrangement will narrow your choices.

Ribbon Styles

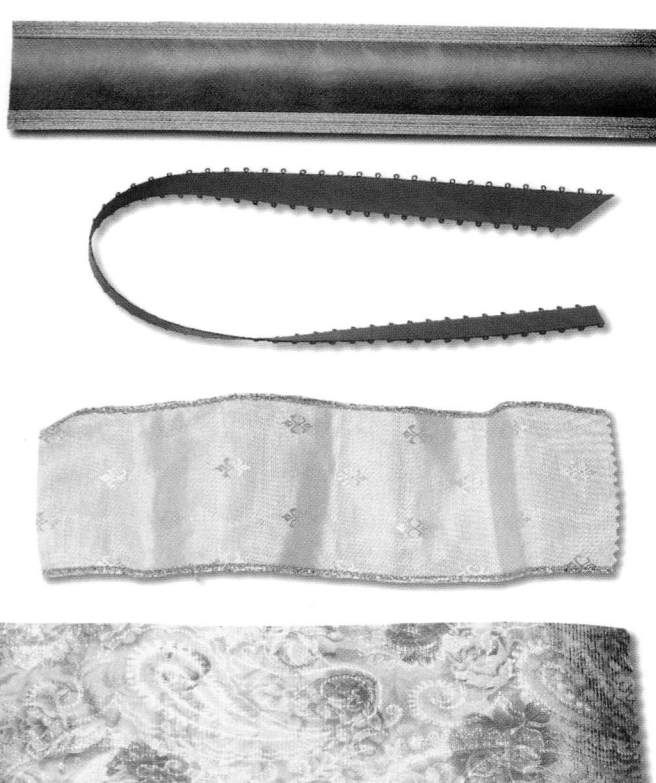

Ribbons are available with different edge treatments; this can be important in design, as some edges will fray with frequent handling. *Woven edge ribbon* has a finished edge which will not fray. This ribbon is easy to use in bows because of its softness and pliability.

Picot ribbon is a woven edge ribbon distinguished by small loops extending outward from each edge. Including picot ribbon with plain ribbons in a multi-ribbon bow adds texture and interest. Picot ribbons add a nice touch to romantic designs.

Wire-edged ribbon is easy to use because it has "memory"; each edge is woven around a thin wire. If a bow becomes crushed it's easy to reshape the loops, making the bow look new. The tails can be rippled and tucked among design components, with the wires holding the shape. The wires can be pulled to easily shirr the ribbon.

Cut edge ribbons are often used in floral work. Less expensive, they are available in many of the same patterns and designs as woven or wire-edged ribbon. To reduce fraying, sizing is added—this stiffens the ribbon, but also means that any creases made in forming the bow will remain visible. Eventually the edges will fray, so handle the ribbon as little as possible.

Paper ribbon has become a floral design staple. Some of these ribbons come twisted into cords and can be used that way, or untwisted to make crinkly flat ribbon. The twisted cords make fun accents twined through and around a bow made from flat paper ribbon. Printed paper ribbons are available both on reels or in packaged lengths. Their patterns are muted, making them nice for dried arrangements. Also available are lacy paper ribbons which resemble eyelet.

Choosing Your Ribbons:

The ribbons you use can determine the entire look of your design. For example, heavy tapestries give a more European look, while narrow satin ribbons add a light, romantic effect. The ribbon should tie the design together and actually become part of it.

In choosing a ribbon, both color and width play important roles. Incompatible colors or textures can produce a jarring effect. Using a ribbon which has many the colors in the design ties the design elements together.

If one ribbon with all the right colors can't be found, use two or three ribbons, each in one of the colors needed, and stack the bows. Make a large bow of the widest ribbon (usually the dominant color in the design), then wire or glue a smaller bow of narrower ribbon to the center of it.

Another method of tying colors together is to make one bow of several different ribbons. Hold them together and handle as if they were one length to make a bow of the desired size and type.

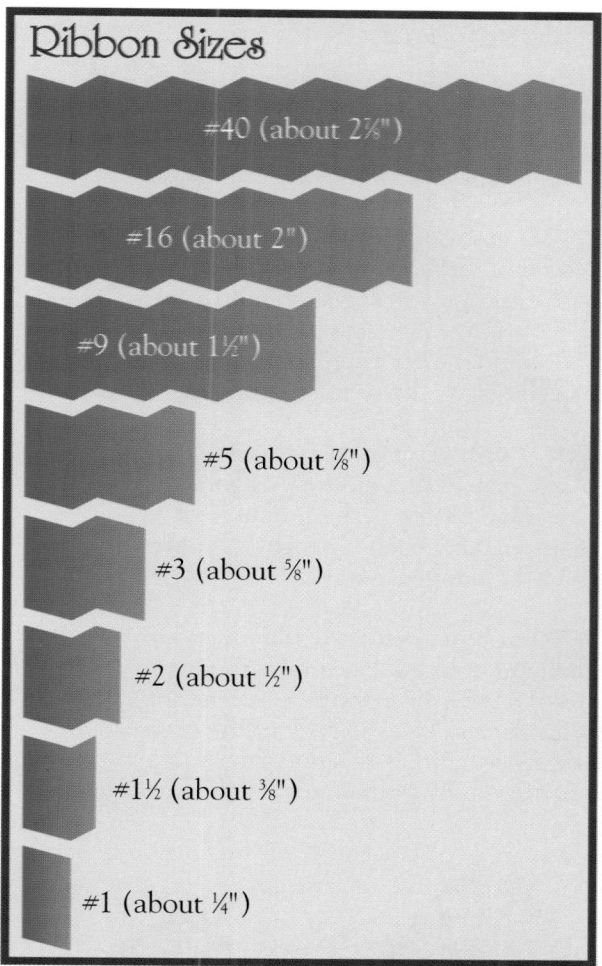

Ribbon Sizes

#40 (about 2⅞")

#16 (about 2")

#9 (about 1½")

#5 (about ⅞")

#3 (about ⅝")

#2 (about ½")

#1½ (about ⅜")

#1 (about ¼")

How Much Do I Need?

Although projects in this book include the yardage needed for each bow in the materials list, you may want to make a different bow. First decide how many loops and tails you want, and how long they will be (if you want a center loop, double its length, add ½" and add this measurement along with the tails.) Then do this easy math:

1. ____" (loop length) x 2 + ½" extra (for the twist) = **A**

2. **A** x (number of loops) = **B**

3. **B** + ____" (tail length) + ____" (tail length) = **C**

4. **C** ÷ 36" = yardage required.

For example:

To make a bow with eight 4" loops, a 6" tail and a 7" tail,

1. 4" x 2" + ½" = 8½"

2. 8½" x 8 loops = **68"**

3. 68" + 6" (tail length) +7" (tail length) = **81"**

4. 81" ÷ 36" = 2.25 or 2¼ yards.

Many times ribbon is used to bring different design elements together visually. This is done by tucking, rippling or looping ribbon lengths or the bow tails among the other materials in the project. Twisting the ribbon as it's looped adds interest. If the base is visible in one area of the design (such as on a vine wreath with all the flowers at the upper left), wrapping the ribbon around the bare areas will help tie the design together. The ribbon draws your eye into the undecorated space and provides continuity.

Other materials such as cord, braid, pearls, beads or wired star garlands can be used with or in place of ribbon.

For wide ribbons a "couched" effect can be achieved by pinching the ribbon every few inches and wrapping the pinched areas with 30-gauge wire. The ribbon will puff between the wires. Glue the wired areas into the design.

Oblong Bow

1 Form a center loop by wrapping the ribbon around your thumb. Twist the ribbon a half turn to keep the right side showing, then make a loop on one side of the center loop.

2 Make another half twist and another loop on the other side. Make another half twist and form a slightly longer loop on each side of your hand; notice these loops are placed diagonally to the first loops.

3 Make two more twists and loops on the opposite diagonal. Continue for the desired number of loops, making each set slightly longer than the previous set.

4 **For tails:** Bring the ribbon end up and hold in place under the bow. Insert a wire through the center loop, bring the ends to the back of the bow, and twist tightly to secure. Trim each tail diagonally or in an inverted V.

Puffy Bow

1 If a center loop is required, begin with one end of the ribbon length and make the center loop. Twist the ribbon to keep the right side showing. If no center loop is called for, begin with step 2.

2 Make a loop on one side of your thumb. Give the ribbon a twist and make another loop, the same length as the first, on the other side of your thumb. Continue making loops and twists until the desired number is reached (a ten-loop bow has five loops on each side), ending with a twist.

3 **For tails:** Bring the ribbon end up and hold in place under the bow, making a long loop (two or more loops can be made for multiple tails). Insert a wire through the center loop, bring the ends to the back of the bow, and twist tightly to secure. Trim each tail diagonally or in an inverted V.

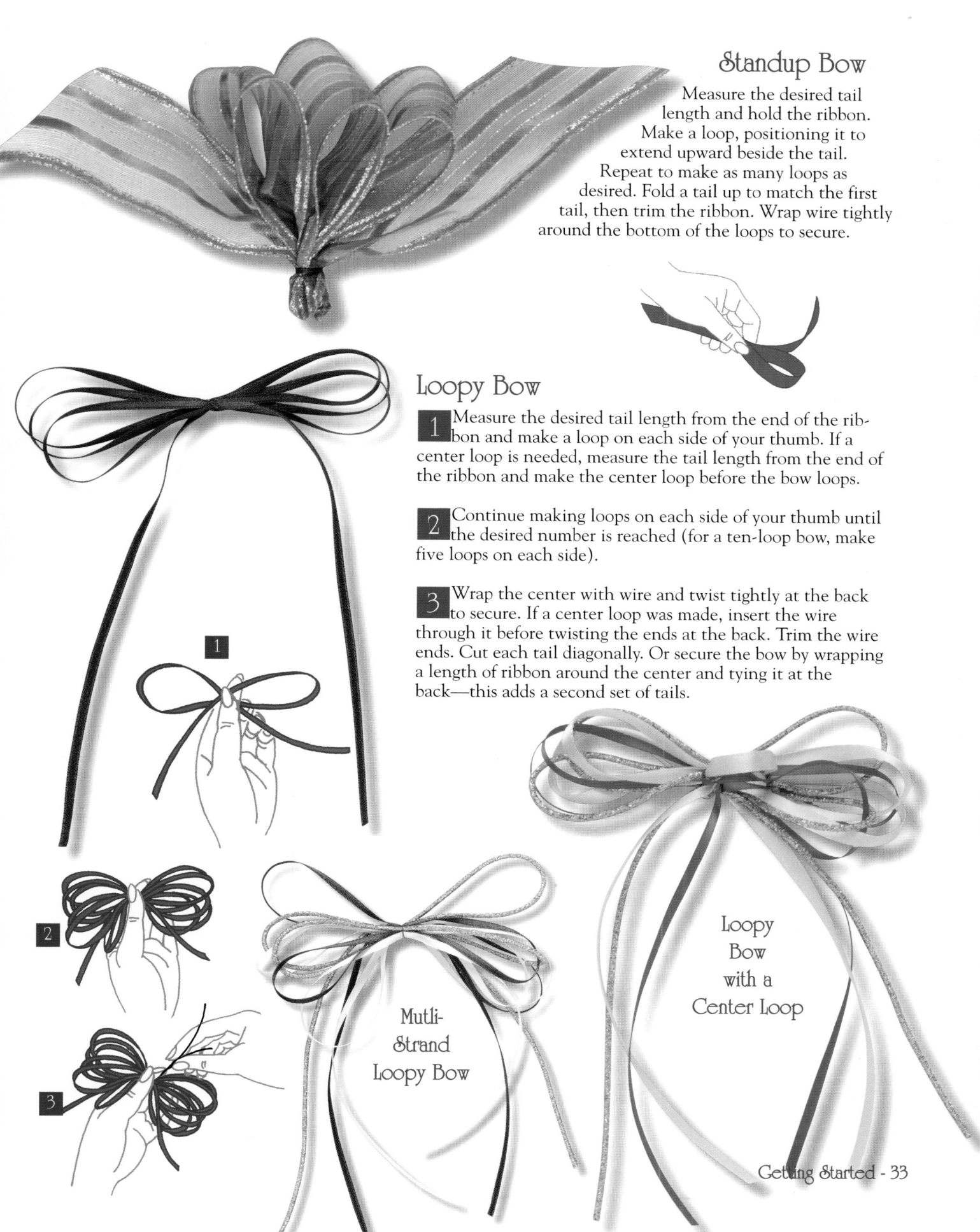

Standup Bow

Measure the desired tail length and hold the ribbon. Make a loop, positioning it to extend upward beside the tail. Repeat to make as many loops as desired. Fold a tail up to match the first tail, then trim the ribbon. Wrap wire tightly around the bottom of the loops to secure.

Loopy Bow

1 Measure the desired tail length from the end of the ribbon and make a loop on each side of your thumb. If a center loop is needed, measure the tail length from the end of the ribbon and make the center loop before the bow loops.

2 Continue making loops on each side of your thumb until the desired number is reached (for a ten-loop bow, make five loops on each side).

3 Wrap the center with wire and twist tightly at the back to secure. If a center loop was made, insert the wire through it before twisting the ends at the back. Trim the wire ends. Cut each tail diagonally. Or secure the bow by wrapping a length of ribbon around the center and tying it at the back—this adds a second set of tails.

Multi-Strand Loopy Bow

Loopy Bow with a Center Loop

Collar Bow

1 Form a ribbon length into a circle, crossing the ends in front. Pinch together, forming a bow, and adjust the loop size and tail length. If no tails are desired, form the length into a circle and just barely overlap the ends before pinching into a bow.

2 Wrap the center with wire and twist tightly at the back to secure. Trim the wire ends, then wrap a short length of ribbon over the center wire and glue the ends at the back. Cut each tail diagonally or in an inverted V.

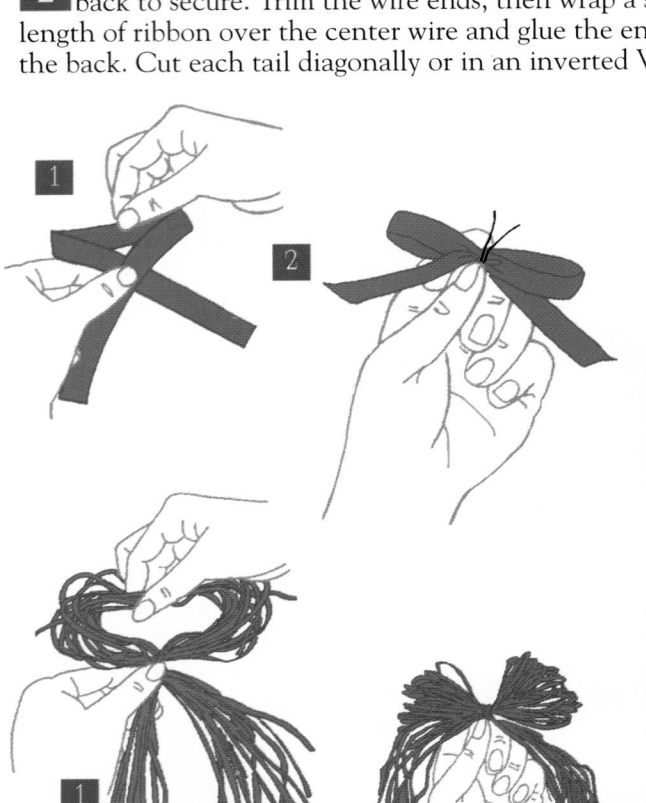

Raffia Collar Bow

1 Hold 20–30 raffia strands together and form them into a circle, crossing the ends at the bottom. Pinch together, forming a bow, and adjust the loop sizes and tail lengths.

2 Tie the center with a raffia strand (a damp raffia strand is stronger); knot it at the back. Blend the ends into the other tails.

Raffia Loopy Bow

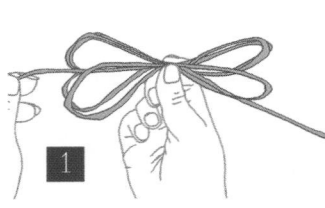

1 Measure the desired tail length from one end of a raffia strand, then make a loop on each side of your thumb.

2 Continue to loop the raffia strand back and forth until all the raffia is used but enough for the opposite tail. Wire to secure, or tie the center with another strand of raffia and knot it at the back to secure. (If a fuller bow is desired, repeat with another strand before securing.)

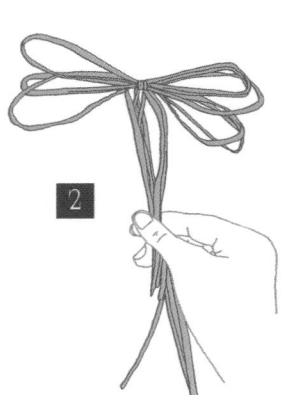

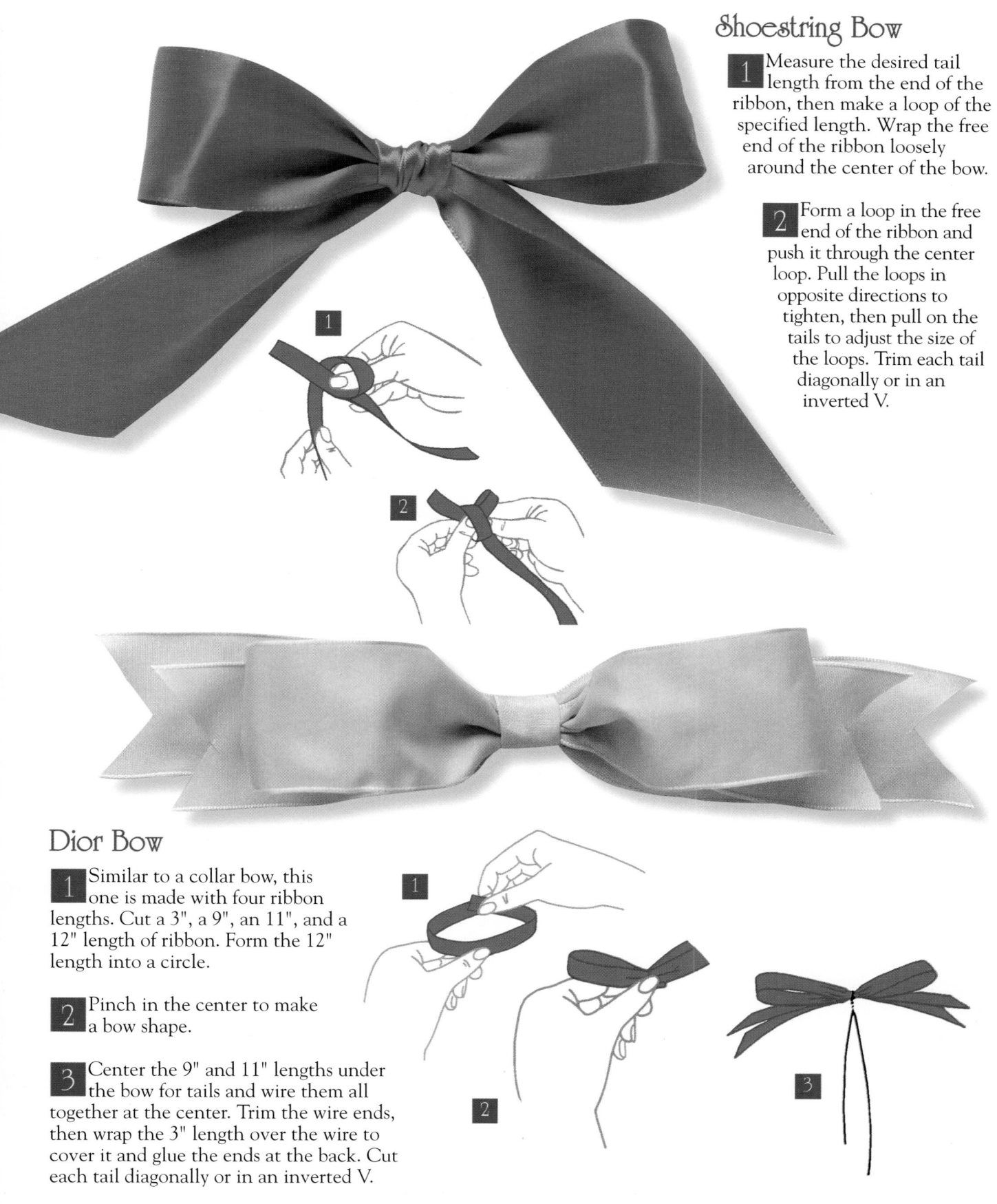

Shoestring Bow

1 Measure the desired tail length from the end of the ribbon, then make a loop of the specified length. Wrap the free end of the ribbon loosely around the center of the bow.

2 Form a loop in the free end of the ribbon and push it through the center loop. Pull the loops in opposite directions to tighten, then pull on the tails to adjust the size of the loops. Trim each tail diagonally or in an inverted V.

Dior Bow

1 Similar to a collar bow, this one is made with four ribbon lengths. Cut a 3", a 9", an 11", and a 12" length of ribbon. Form the 12" length into a circle.

2 Pinch in the center to make a bow shape.

3 Center the 9" and 11" lengths under the bow for tails and wire them all together at the center. Trim the wire ends, then wrap the 3" length over the wire to cover it and glue the ends at the back. Cut each tail diagonally or in an inverted V.

Winning Wreaths

Wreaths are one of the most popular floral home decor items, whether displayed on the front door as a cheery welcome or as a decorative accent over a fireplace. Dried flowers are a perfect complement to wreaths because the materials are easy to use and long-lasting.

A small selection of blossoms can be used for a simple and charming look like the Lavender Bouquet Wreath (page 51), or an abundance of flowers can be gathered to create an opulent, lush design like the Garden Wreath with Lavender (page 38). Keeping the design style and its size in mind when choosing the materials will ensure perfect results.

Today, wreath bases come in many different shapes—hearts, ovals and square wreaths are available in a variety of sizes. The materials from which the wreaths are created range from exotic roots, cornhusks, branches and barks to more common vines and twigs, with finishes varying from bleached to lacquered and painted.

Because of the fascinating textures and appearances of many wreaths, just a small amount of decoration is needed to create an exciting finished piece. Crescent floral designs are especially applicable in this case, as they can created in a variety of positions on the wreath and sized to cover as much of it as desired. When choosing a wreath base, decide whether it should be exposed as part of the design. If so, maybe it can be incorporated into the design by being partially covered with materials, or maybe pieces of the wreath can be pulled into the components, providing unity.

Wreaths are very versatile and popular, and gathering the materials to for a wreath to fit that special place in a home can be exciting and fun. The many examples we've provided here will spark ideas and creativity for some beautiful designs.

Garden Wreath with Lavender

one 18″ round grapevine wreath
6 oz. of sage green dried mini millet
4 oz. of pink dried larkspur
3 oz. of yellow dried solidago
6 oz. of white dried button flowers
3 oz. of blue dried echinops
8 oz. of purple preserved lavender

ten 6″ wide purple/green dried hydrangea blossom
   heads
two 4″ wide pink preserved hydrangea blossom
   heads
six 2″ wide pink preserved roses
three 3½″ wide pink freeze-dried gardenias
22-gauge wire, low temperature glue gun and sticks

1 Attach a wire hanger (see page 26) to the wreath top back. Cut the purple hydrangea into 3″–4″ wide clusters and glue evenly spaced around the wreath as shown. Cut the millet into 5″–6″ sprigs and glue them in clusters of 4–5 among the hydrangeas, alternating the angles from inside to outside. Repeat with the larkspur.

2 Cut the solidago into 5″ sprigs and glue them evenly spaced around the wreath, angling some sprigs clockwise and some counterclockwise. Divide the button flowers into three equal groups and wire each group 3″ below the blossoms; cut the stems off just below the wire. Glue one group at 12:30, one at 5:00 and one at 8:00.

3 Cut the echinops into 4″ sprigs. Glue three to the inner edge at 1:00 and five to the inner edge at 9:00. Glue five to the outer edge at 4:00. Glue the roses evenly spaced around the wreath.

4 Cut the lavender into 7″ sprigs and divide them into five equal bunches. Wire each bunch together just under the blossoms, then fan them slightly by pulling the stems in opposite directions. Glue the bunches evenly spaced around the wreath, angled as shown in the large photo. Glue the gardenias to the wreath front at 1:30, 5:30 and 9:00. Cut the pink hydrangea into 3″ sprigs and glue them around the wreath to fill in sparse areas.

Manzanita Wreath

one 20" round manzanita wreath
10 stems of pink dried roses
four 4"–5" wide greenish-blue dried hydrangea
    blossom heads
3 oz. of green preserved plumosus fern
2 oz. of pink preserved leptospermum
2 oz. of white dried starflowers
2 oz. of dark blue dried larkspur
3 oz. of dried avena
6" of 22-gauge wire
low temperature glue gun and sticks

1 Attach a wire hanger (see page 26) to the wreath top back. Cut the fern into 6"–8" sprigs and glue them evenly spaced around the wreath, following the angles of the manzanita leaves. Cut the roses to 8" long and glue them alternately near the inside and outside edges of the wreath, angled clockwise.

2 Cut the leptospermum into 5"–8" sprigs and glue them as for the roses. Cut the starflowers into 5"–6" sprigs and glue them in clusters of 12–15 alternately near the inside and outside edges of the wreath.

3 Cut the larkspur into 6"–8" sprigs and glue them evenly spaced around the wreath, angled as for the leptospermum. Cut the hydrangea heads into 2"–4" sprigs and glue them among the previous materials, filling any large open areas.

4 Cut the avena into 8" sprigs. Glue in pairs evenly spaced around the outside of the wreath, angled clockwise. Glue the remaining sprigs singly, evenly spaced among the previous materials.

Log Birdhouse Wreath

one 14" round grapevine wreath
one 4"x5½" log birdhouse
one 2" wide dried pomegranate
six 1"–2" wide mini lotus pods on stems
two 2" long blue/pink mushroom birds
4 oz. of golden brown preserved oak leaves
3 oz. of dried mini millet
3 oz. of dried birch or buck twigs
2 oz. of preserved baby's breath
2 oz. of blue dried echinops
2 oz. of pink dried pepperberries
2 oz. of green sphagnum moss
6" of 22-gauge wire
low temperature glue gun and sticks

1 Attach a wire hanger (see page 26) to the wreath top back. Glue the moss in a crescent around the left half and bottom of the wreath. Glue the birdhouse to the inside bottom. Cut the oak leaves into 3"–4" sprigs and glue them into the moss, angling the leaves away from the 7:30 position.

2 Cut the millet into 4"–6" sprigs and glue them among the oak leaves at similar angles. Cut the twigs into 5"–10" lengths. Glue them among the leaves, angled as for the leaves but slightly more forward.

3 Glue the pomegranate at 7:30. Cut the lotus pods to 5" long. Glue one below the right side of the birdhouse, extending forward. Glue one between the pomegranate and the right lotus pod. Glue one left of the pomegranate extending forward, then glue three more 2"–3" apart up the left side of the wreath, alternating them first right, then left, then right again as shown.

4 Cut the baby's breath into 4" sprigs and glue them evenly spaced throughout the design. Cut the echinops and the pepperberries into 3" sprigs and glue them evenly spaced among the lotus pods. Glue one bird to a twig right of the pomegranate and the other to the top of the birdhouse.

Birch Wreath with Sunflowers

one 30" round birch twig wreath
6 oz. of dried bay leaf branches
3 oz. of white dried baby everlastings
4 oz. of purple preserved ti tree
three 2½"–3" dried sunflowers
four 1½"–2" dried sunflowers
4 oz. of yellow dried solidago
3 oz. of dried ambrosinia
4 oz. of dark plum preserved sinuata
    statice
3 oz. of dried caspia
2 oz. of dried festuca grass
22-gauge wire
low temperature glue gun and sticks

1 Attach a wire hanger (see page 26) to the top back of the wreath. Cut the bay leaves into 6"–12" sprigs and glue them evenly spaced among the birch twigs, angled in the same directions. Cut the baby everlastings and ti tree into 8"–12" sprigs and glue them evenly spaced among the bay leaves and twigs at similar angles.

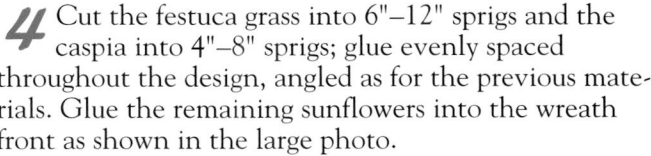

4 Cut the festuca grass into 6"–12" sprigs and the caspia into 4"–8" sprigs; glue evenly spaced throughout the design, angled as for the previous materials. Glue the remaining sunflowers into the wreath front as shown in the large photo.

2 Glue the three largest sunflowers in a triangle around the inside edge of the wreath. Cut the solidago into 5"–10" sprigs and glue them throughout the design, angled as for the bay leaves and alternating from inside to outside.

3 Cut ⅔ of the ambrosinia into 10" sprigs and glue them evenly spaced extending to the outer edge of the wreath, angled as for the bay. Cut the remaining ambrosinia into 6" sprigs and glue around the inside edge of the wreath, angled in the same directions. Cut the statice into 4" sprigs and glue evenly spaced throughout the design.

Double Heart Wreath

grapevine heart wreaths: one 20", one 10" wide
five 2" wide white freeze-dried roses
4 oz. of green preserved plumosus fern
3 oz. of white dried ixodia daisies
3 oz. of mauve preserved heather
4 oz. of preserved green pepperberry foliage with many
   clusters of red berries
3 oz. of mauve preserved misty limonium
4½ yards of 1½" wide dark mauve satin ribbon
22-gauge wire
low temperature glue gun and sticks

1 Wire the wreaths together as shown. Hold one end of the ribbon at the inside top left of the large wreath and wrap it spiral fashion all the way around, positioning the wraps 4"–5" apart. At the top, continue winding the ribbon around the small wreath. Glue the ends of the ribbon on the back to secure. Make a wire hanger (see page 26) on the top back.

2 Cut the plumosus into 4"–6" sprigs and glue them to extend from under the ribbon wraps as shown, leaving the bottom of each wreath empty. Glue a rose to the center top of the large wreath; glue another 5" away on each side. Glue the last two to the small wreath as shown.

3 Cut the daisies into 4"–6" sprigs. Glue a few sprigs to each side of the large wreath, angled downward, extending to 7:00 on the left and to 3:00 on the right. Glue the rest evenly spaced around the roses, angled to the sides, with the center sprigs angled forward. Cut the heather into 5"–7" sprigs and glue as for the daisies.

4 Cut the pepperberries into 5"–7" sprigs and glue them evenly spaced among the materials in the top half of the wreath, at similar angles. Cut the limonium into 5"–8" sprigs and glue them evenly spaced among the daisies and heather.

Hydrangea Wreath

one 14" round grapevine wreath
ten 4"–5" wide lavender/blue preserved
    hydrangea blossom heads
three 1½"–2" wide pink preserved roses
2 oz. of dried twigs
2 oz. of white dried German statice
2 oz. of white preserved sinuata statice
2 oz. of pink preserved leptospermum
3 oz. of purple preserved lavender
2 oz. of green preserved isolepsis grass
22-gauge wire
low temperature glue gun and sticks

1 Attach a wire hanger (see page 26) to the wreath top back. Cut the hydrangea into 2"–3" wide clusters. Fluff each cluster by pulling it slightly apart. Set aside three 3" clusters for step 4. Glue the rest around the wreath, covering it completely.

2 Cut the twigs into 5"–7" sprigs and glue them to the wreath angling away from the 10:00 position as shown. Cut the German statice into 3"–4" sprigs. Glue half between 10:00 and 12:00 angled upward and half between 10:00 to 9:00 angled downward.

3 Cut the leptospermum into 4"–7" sprigs and glue them among the twigs, angled and spaced the same way. Cut the rose stems to 1" long. Glue a rose at 10:00, one at 12:00 and one at 9:00. Cut the sinuata statice into 3" sprigs and glue them evenly spaced among the roses and leptospermum.

4 Cut the lavender into 4"–6" sprigs and glue in clusters of 2–4 evenly spaced among the statice and leptospermum. Cut the isolepsis grass into 6"–9" sprigs and glue as for the lavender. Glue the three hydrangea clusters from step 1 evenly spaced throughout the design area as shown in the large photo.

Romantic Heart Wreath

one 16" lacquered grapevine heart wreath
5 stems of pink dried roses, ¾" wide
2 oz. of white dried German statice
2 oz. of light green dwarf's beard moss
2 oz. of light green preserved lepidium
2 oz. of dark pink preserved heather
2 oz. of dried lavender
3 oz. of white preserved rice flowers
2⅔ yards of ⅝" wide mauve taffeta wire-
*   edged ribbon*
22-gauge wire
low temperature glue gun and sticks

1 Attach a wire hanger (see page 26) to the top back of the wreath. Cut the German statice into 3" sprigs. Glue ⅔ of them to the upper left heart shoulder, radiating outward from the center of the curve. Glue the remaining sprigs at the bottom right extending in both directions along the wreath. Break the moss into 2" tufts and glue them among the statice sprigs.

2 Use the ribbon to make an oblong bow (see page 32) with two 2¼" loops, two 2¾" loops, six 3" loops and 18" tails; trim each tail in an inverted "V." Glue the bow to the center of the upper statice. Cross the tails 5" from the ends and glue in the center of the lower statice. Cut the roses to 2" long. Glue one at the bow center and one 4" away on each side of the bow. Glue the last two to the crossed area of the tails.

3 Cut the lepidium into 4"–6" sprigs and glue them evenly spaced throughout the design, following the angles of the previous materials. Cut the heather into 2"–6" sprigs. Glue two or three 2" sprigs on each side of the lower roses. Glue the rest of the sprigs among the lepidium sprigs in the upper design area.

4 Cut the lavender into 3"–6" sprigs and glue as for the lepidium. Cut the rice flowers into 2"–3" sprigs; glue them evenly spaced around the roses and the bow.

White Rose Wreath

one 12" round grapevine wreath
5 white preserved roses, 2"–3" wide
3 oz. of green preserved plumosus fern
2 oz. of dried ivy
2 oz. of green preserved bracken fern
2 oz. of green preserved austral fern
2 oz. of light green preserved ming fern
2 oz. of green preserved hanging
  amaranthus
3 oz. of green preserved misty limonium
2 oz. of white preserved rice flowers
2 oz. of white dried larkspur
1⅛ yards of 1⅜" wide green ombré taffeta
  wire-edged ribbon
22-gauge wire
low temperature glue gun and sticks

1 Attach a wire hanger to the top back of the wreath. Cut the plumosus into 6"–8" sprigs and glue them evenly spaced over the wreath as shown, allowing some sprigs to trail over the outside edge of the wreath. Cut the ivy into 4"–6" sprigs and glue them 2"–3" apart among the plumosus.

2 Cut the bracken and austral fern into 4"–5" sprigs and glue them among the other greens, angled counterclockwise. Glue a rose to the center top of the wreath. Glue the remaining four roses staggered down the right side, 1½"–2" apart and extending forward.

3 Cut the amaranthus into 6"–12" sprigs. Glue 2–3 shorter sprigs under the second rose from the bottom and the rest under and left of the lowest rose, all angled downward. Cut the limonium into 3"–6" sprigs and glue a 6" sprig under the lowest rose, angled downward. Glue the rest evenly spaced among the roses, angled upward and outward.

4 Use the ribbon to make a puffy bow (see page 32) with four 3" loops and 6" tails; trim each tail in an inverted "V." Glue the bow under the lowest rose. Cut the ming fern and larkspur into 4" sprigs and the rice flowers into 3" sprigs; glue them evenly spaced among the roses, extending forward.

Cornhusk Wreath with Oranges

one 15" round cornhusk wreath
1¾"–2½" wide whole dried oranges: 1 orange,
   2 green
five 2" wide yellow/brown dried sunflowers
3 oz. of dried barley
2 oz. of dried oats
3 oz. of green dried hops
3 oz. of dried setaria
2 oz. of 60" long raffia
22-gauge wire
low temperature glue gun and sticks

1 Attach a wire hanger (see page 26) to the top back of the wreath. Cut the barley into 4"–7" sprigs and wire them together in three equal clusters. Cut the oats into 8" sprigs, and wire together in two clusters. Glue a barley cluster at 9:00 and one at 8:00, both angled upward and toward the inside of the wreath. Glue the third at 8:00 angled outward. Glue an oats cluster at 9:00 and one at 10:00, both angled upward.

2 Use the raffia to make a collar bow (see page 34) with 4" loops and 22" tails. Glue it at an angle below the lowest barley clusters. Cut a 7" hops sprig and glue it below the bow extending downward. Cut the remaining hops into 4" sprigs and glue them evenly spaced among the barley and oats sprigs.

3 Glue the oranges to the bow center as shown. Glue a sunflower among the hops 2" below the oranges. Glue the remaining sunflowers evenly spaced among the materials above the bow, angling them alternately toward the outside and inside.

4 Cut the setaria into 4"–8" sprigs. Glue them evenly spaced among the florals above and below the bow at similar angles to the previous materials.

Harvest Spiral Wreath

one 24" round spiral twig wreath
three 2½"–3" wide dried lotus pods
5 stems of brown lacquered dried papaver
4 oz. of burgundy preserved eucalyptus
4 oz. of yellow/brown preserved oak
  leaves
2 oz. of red preserved oak leaves
3 oz. of orange preserved myrtle
2 oz. of dried tulyp star
4 oz. of yellow dried caspia
2 oz. of raffia, 30" long
22-gauge wire
low temperature glue gun and sticks

1 Attach a wire hanger (see page 26) to the top back of the wreath. Lay the wreath on your worktable so the twigs angle counterclockwise. Cut the eucalyptus into eight 8" and eight 6" sprigs. Glue them evenly spaced around the wreath, alternating 8" and 6" sprigs, angling them in the same direction as the twigs. Cut the yellow/brown oak leaves into 4"–8" sprigs; glue them around the wreath as shown.

2 Cut the myrtle into 4"–8" sprigs and glue them evenly around the wreath, placing shorter sprigs in front. Cut the tulyp star into 3"–9" sprigs. Separate into five equal bunches, each with sprigs of all lengths, and glue evenly spaced around the wreath.

3 Cut the caspia into 4"–8" sprigs and glue them among the florals, angled in the same manner, with shorter sprigs in front. Cut a 7" raffia length and set aside. Hold the rest together to make a loopy bow (see page 34) with 4" loops and 9" tails; tie with the 7" strand. Glue it at 4:00 and drape the tails to the left as shown. Separate the bow loops into three sections; glue the lotus pods between the bow loops.

4 Cut the papaver stems to 4" long. Glue one in the bow center and two on each side of the bow. Cut the red oak leaves into 3"–6" sprigs. Glue the longer sprigs evenly spaced around the wreath and the shorter ones among the bow loops, lotus and papaver.

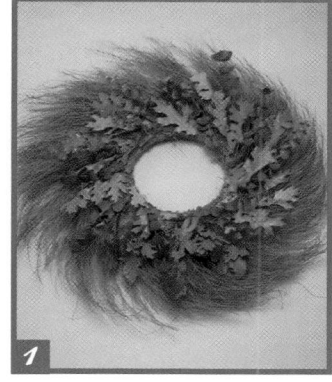

Peaches &
Cream

one 13" round lacquered grapevine wreath
three 3" wide peach freeze-dried roses
2 stems of peach silk vervain, each with three 4" long
   blossom spikes
4 oz. of green preserved oak leaves
2 oz. of green preserved misty limonium
2 oz. of white sinuata statice
2 oz. of light green preserved ti tree
peach spray paint for florals
2⅜ yards of sage green taffeta ribbon with peach wired edges
22-gauge wire, low temperature glue gun and sticks

1 Attach a wire hanger (see page 26) to the top back
of the wreath. Cut the oak leaves into 4"–6" sprigs.
Glue a few at the top center, angled upward and down.
Glue the rest on each side, extending to 3:00 and 8:00.
Cut the limonium into 4"–6" sprigs and glue them
among the oak leaves at similar angles.

2 Use the ribbon to make an oblong bow (see page
32) with two 3½" loops, four 4" loops and 18" tails.
Glue it to the top center of the wreath. Loop and glue
one tail down each side. Glue a rose to the bow center
and one on each side of the bow.

3 Cut the statice into 2"–3" sprigs and divide into
two bunches; spray one bunch peach and let dry.
Set the peach statice aside for step 4. Cut the ti tree
into 4"–6" sprigs. Glue the ti and white statice evenly
spaced among the florals and bow loops.

4 Glue the peach statice evenly spaced among the
white statice and ti tree. Cut the blossom spikes off
the vervain. Glue one on each side of the upper bow
loops, gently bending it into a downward curve. Glue a
sprig to extend from under the lower bow loops on each
side of the wreath, curving below the side roses. Glue
one to extend from under under the center of each bow
tail, curving it to follow the wreath shape.

Dried Garden Wreath

one 12" round grapevine wreath
12 stems of pink dried roses, ¾" wide
one 6"–7" wide pink dried hydrangea blossom head
4 oz. of white dried German statice
3 oz. of ivory preserved sinuata statice
4 oz. of white dried ammobium
2 oz. of pink dried ti tree
2 oz. of lavender preserved peppergrass
1¼ yards of 1⅜" wide lavender organza ribbon
22-gauge wire, low temperature glue gun and sticks

1 Attach a wire hanger (see page 26) to the top back of the wreath. Cut the German statice into 4" sprigs. Glue them around the outside and inside of the wreath, angled counterclockwise. Cut the ammobium into 3" sprigs and glue in clusters of 10–15, spaced 1"–2" apart and alternating from inside to outside as shown.

2 Cut the roses to 3" long and glue them among the ammobium sprigs, extending forward. Cut the hydrangea into 2"–3" wide clusters and glue them throughout the design, alternating them from inside to outside.

3 Cut the sinuata statice into 3" sprigs and glue them among the other florals to conceal the remaining bare areas. Cut the ti tree into 4" sprigs and glue clusters of 2–4 counterclockwise, evenly spaced among the previous materials.

4 Cut the peppergrass into 3"–4" sprigs and glue them among the other materials. Tuck one end of the ribbon into the wreath center top. Weave it gently among the florals, tucking and gluing it deep into the sprigs every 3"–5" around the wreath.

Imperial Rose Wreath

one 10" round grapevine wreath
eight 2" wide red preserved roses
6 oz. of green preserved salal
2 oz. of gold dried curly twigs
3 oz. of purple preserved lavender
3 oz. of maroon preserved sinuata statice
3 oz. of pink preserved heather
2 oz. of red preserved leptospermum
2 oz. of pink preserved rice flowers
22-gauge wire
low temperature glue gun and sticks

1 Attach a wire hanger (see page 26) to the top back of the wreath. Cut the salal into 3"–5" sprigs with two to five leaves each. Glue one to the wreath, angled counterclockwise and slightly toward the outside edge. Glue the next one angled to the inside edge, then glue a third angled over the center of the wreath to cover the exposed wreath between the first two sprigs. Continue around the wreath to completely cover it.

2 Cut the heather and ti tree into 4"–6" sprigs and glue them evenly spaced, angled counterclockwise. Cut the rice flowers into 3" sprigs and glue them evenly spaced throughout the design, angled forward.

3 Glue the roses evenly spaced around the wreath, alternating from inside to outside. Cut the twigs into 4" sprigs and glue them evenly spaced among the salal leaves.

4 Cut the lavender into 4"–6" sprigs and wire into clusters of 5–8 sprigs. Glue them to the wreath angled counterclockwise, alternating from inner to outer edge. Cut the statice into 3" sprigs and glue them evenly spaced throughout the design.

Lavender Bouquet Wreath

one 12" round woven bleached willow
   wreath
6 stems of pink dried roses, ¾" wide
4 oz. of dried lavender
2 oz. of white dried larkspur
2 oz. of green dried silene
⅞ yard of 1½" wide green/peach ombré
   taffeta wire-edged ribbon
22-gauge wire
low temperature glue gun and sticks

1 Attach a wire hanger (see page
   26) to the top back of the wreath.
Gather the lavender, holding it just under the heads.
Pull some of the back stems upward and some of the
front stems downward to form a multi-layered bouquet.
Wire the bouquet below the front heads. Wrap the ribbon over the wire and tie in a shoestring bow (see page
35) with 2½" loops and 8" tails. Trim the stems so the
finished bouquet is 18" long.

2 Wire the bouquet to the wreath with the blossoms
   at 2:00 and the stems at 6:00. Cut the larkspur into
2"–4" sprigs and glue them to the center of the bow
extending forward and up.

3 Remove the leaves from the rose stems. Cut the
   roses to 2"–3" long. Glue the leaves and roses
evenly spaced among the larkspur sprigs.

4 Cut the silene into 2"–6" sprigs. Glue them evenly
   spaced throughout the roses and larkspur.

Salal & Bay Wreath

one 10" round grapevine wreath
12 stems of yellow dried roses, ¾" wide
6 oz. of dried salal leaves
2 oz. of green dried bay leaf branches
2 oz. of dried ambrosinia
2 oz. of white dried sinuata statice
2 oz. of green dried silene grass
2 oz. of white dried larkspur
22-gauge wire
low temperature glue gun and sticks

1 Attach a wire hanger (see page 26) to the top back of the wreath. Cut the salal into 3"–6" sprigs of 2–5 leaves each. Glue the sprigs extending counterclockwise and covering the entire wreath.

2 Cut the ambrosinia into 5" sprigs and glue them in clusters of 2–3 evenly spaced among the salal leaves at similar angles. Cut the roses to 4" long and glue them in pairs evenly spaced around the wreath, angled as for the ambrosinia.

3 Cut the statice into 3" sprigs and glue them evenly spaced throughout the design. Cut the silene grass into 4"–5" sprigs and glue in clusters of 2–3 among the other florals, filling any bare spaces, particularly around the outside edge.

4 Cut the bay leaves into 3"–6" sprigs and glue them evenly spaced among the other florals, extending slightly forward. Cut the larkspur into 3"–6" sprigs and glue as for the bay leaves.

Wreath with Chilies

one 10" round wire
  wreath form with
  10 clamps
3 oz. of dried bay
  leaf branches
3 oz. of dried avena
3 oz. of blue dried
  larkspur
2 oz. of red pre-
  served bracken
  fern
2 oz. of dried nigella
3 oz. of white dried
  ti tree
3 oz. of red dried
  chilies on stems
2 oz. of dried linum
2 oz. of raffia, 28" long
22-gauge wire
low temperature glue gun and sticks

1 Cut the bay leaves and avena into 7" sprigs. Cut the larkspur and fern into 5" sprigs. Cut the nigella into 3"–4" sprigs. Hold two bay, four avena, two larkspur, two fern and four nigella sprigs together and wire them at the stem ends as shown. Repeat to make ten mixed bouquets.

2 Lay a bouquet between the wire clamps on the wreath frame, stems to the left, and squeeze the clamps together, overlapping the ends behind the wreath frame to secure the bouquet tightly. Lay the next bouquet between the clamps to the left of the first, covering the first stems, and secure. Repeat around the wreath.

3 Attach a wire hanger (see page 26) to the top back of the wreath. Cut the ti tree into 3"–6" sprigs and glue them evenly spaced around the wreath, angled clockwise, alternating from inside to outside edges. Cut the chilies into 4"–6" sprigs and glue as for the ti tree.

4 Cut half the linum into 9" sprigs and the rest into 3"–6" sprigs. Glue the 9" sprigs around the wreath to extend from behind the bouquets, angled clockwise. Glue the 3"–6" sprigs evenly spaced throughout the design. Shred the raffia strands with your fingernail. Cut six strands to 9" and bend in half to form a loop; wire the ends. Repeat for a total of seven raffia loops. Glue them evenly spaced throughout the design, angled as for the previous materials.

Double Wreath & Swag

round grapevine wreaths: one 12", one 17"
4 oz. of green preserved eucalyptus
3 oz. of dried avena
3 oz. of white dried German statice
2 oz. of pink dried strawflowers
2 oz. of white dried larkspur
3 oz. of blue dried hill flowers
3½ yards of 1⅜" wide blue/white gingham taffeta wire-edged ribbon
3 yards of 1½" wide mauve taffeta wire-edged ribbon
22-gauge wire, low temperature glue gun and sticks

1 Cut 50" of gingham ribbon and glue one end to the bottom front of the 12" wreath. Wrap the ribbon spiral fashion around the wreath, placing the wraps 4" apart; glue to secure the ends. Cut the eucalyptus into 6"–12" sprigs and glue to the wreath bottom, extending from the center beyond the sides as shown.

2 Use the rest of the gingham ribbon to make an oblong bow (see page 32) with a center loop, two 2½" loops, four 3" loops, four 3½" loops and 6" tails; trim each tail in an inverted "V." Glue to the center bottom. Cut the avena into 5"–6" sprigs and glue them among the eucalyptus sprigs, angled and spaced the same.

3 Cut the statice into 4"–6" sprigs and glue them as for the avena. Cut the strawflowers with 2" stems and glue evenly spaced across the swag.

4 Cut the larkspur and hill flowers into 4"–9" sprigs and glue as for the avena. Cut 25" of mauve ribbon and use to make a puffy bow with a center loop, two 2½" loops and 6" tails. Glue it to the center of the gingham bow. Wrap the rest of the mauve ribbon spiral-fashion around the 17" wreath, placing the wraps 6"–7" apart. Wire the 12" wreath inside the bottom of the 17" wreath. Attach a wire hanger (see page 26) to the top back of the 17" wreath.

Herbal Wreath

one 10" round grapevine wreath
6 oz. of green dried bay leaf branches
3 oz. of dried avena
2 oz. of dried ambrosinia
3 oz. of white dried baby everlastings
3 oz. of purple/green dried oregano
4 oz. of lavender dried pennyroyal
2 oz. of dried nigella
22-gauge wire
low temperature glue gun and sticks

1 Attach a wire hanger (see page 26) to the top back of the wreath. Cut fifteen 4" sprigs of bay leaves and glue them evenly spaced around the outside of the wreath, angled counterclockwise. Cut the remaining bay into individual leaves and glue them around the inside and front of the wreath, also counterclockwise.

2 Cut the avena into 4"–6" sprigs and glue them in clusters of three angled counterclockwise around the wreath, filling in the bare spots. Cut the ambrosinia into 4"–6" sprigs and glue them evenly spaced among the avena sprigs, angled in the same manner. Repeat with the baby everlastings.

3 Cut the oregano into 3"–5" sprigs, divide them into five equal clusters and glue them evenly spaced around the wreath, angled counterclockwise. Cut the pennyroyal into 4"–7" sprigs and glue in clusters of 8–10 sprigs between the oregano clusters.

4 Cut the nigella into 2"–4" sprigs and glue them evenly spaced in clusters of three, alternating between the inside and outside wreath edges.

Lace Twig Heart Wreath

one 17" wide TWIGS™ lace heart wreath
5 stems of pink dried roses, ¾"–1" wide
twelve 1"–1½" white dried acroclineum heads
4 oz. of green preserved boxwood
3 oz. of green preserved plumosus fern
3 oz. of pink preserved leptospermum
2 oz. of dried silene grass
2 oz. of green dried rice grass
1⅞ yards of ⅞" wide pink/green variegated taffeta wire-edged ribbon
22-gauge wire
low temperature glue gun and sticks

1 Cut the boxwood into 4"–6" sprigs and glue the longer sprigs to the lower left side of the wreath, extending both directions from 7:30. Glue the shorter sprigs in a layer over the first, angling them slightly forward. Cut the fern into 4"–7" sprigs and glue among the boxwood sprigs at similar angles.

2 Use the ribbon to make a puffy bow (see page 32) with a center loop, eight 2½" loops and 12" tails. Glue it at 7:30; weave one tail upward and one downward among the greens. Cut the roses to 4". Glue one at each end of the floral design. Glue the other three roses in a triangle around the bow as shown.

3 Cut the leptospermum into 3"–6" sprigs and glue them throughout the design as for the plumosus. Cut the acroclineum with 2" stems and glue evenly spaced among the other materials.

4 Cut the silene grass and rice grass into 4"–6" sprigs and glue them as for the plumosus and leptospermum.

Hydrangea Garden Wreath

one 14" round grapevine
  wreath
12–14 assorted 6" wide dried
  hydrangea blossom heads
15 stems of dried papaver
6 oz. of dried birch twigs
4 oz. of dried salal
6 oz. of white preserved rice
  flowers
4 oz. of dried avena
4 oz. of dried caspia
22-gauge wire
low temperature glue gun and
  sticks

1 Attach a wire hanger (see page 26) to the top back of the wreath. Cut the salal into 5"–10" sprigs and glue them angled counterclockwise and slightly forward around the wreath. Cut the birch twigs to 5"–14" long and glue as for the salal.

2 Cut the hydrangea heads into 2"–4" wide clusters. Glue them evenly spaced among the salal leaves, varying the colors.

3 Cut the papaver stems to 5"–6" long. Glue three in a triangle at the center bottom. Repeat evenly spaced around the wreath. Cut the rice flowers into 4"–6" sprigs and glue them evenly spaced among the hydrangeas, extending forward.

4 Cut the avena into 8" sprigs and glue them among the previous materials, angled counterclockwise, with several sprigs around the outer edge. Cut the caspia into 6"–8" sprigs and glue them among the florals, filling any sparse areas.

Wreath on a Fence

one 13"x9" unfinished pine picket fence
one 10" wide bleached willow wreath
terra cotta pots: one 3½" wide, two 1¾" wide
3" terra cotta garden tools: 1 clippers, 1 trowel
one 2"x3" painted wood garden sign
2 oz. of green sheet moss
2 oz. of pink dried spray roses, ¼"–½" wide
2 oz. of white dried ammobium
2 oz. of purple dried oregano
2 oz. of green preserved misty limonium
one 4"x4"x6" block of floral foam for drieds
22-gauge wire
low temperature glue gun and sticks

1 Attach a wire hanger (see page 26) to the top back of the fence. Glue the wreath to the center of the fence. Glue the 3½" terra cotta pot upright inside the bottom of the wreath; glue a 1¾" pot on each side of it, angled as shown. Cut the foam to fit the pots and insert a piece in each.

2 Tuck tufts of moss around the foam in the pots and around the base of the pots. Glue the rest around the wreath. Cut the roses into 2"–3" sprigs and glue ⅔ of them into the left pot. Glue three small clusters to the left wreath, two to the right wreath and one between the center and right pots.

3 Cut the ammobium into 2"–3" sprigs and glue some into the left side of the center pot, some to the front center of the right pot and the rest across the lower half of the wreath as shown. Cut the oregano into 2"–4" sprigs. Glue the longer sprigs into the center pot and the shorter sprigs evenly spaced across the lower half of the wreath.

4 Cut the limonium into 2"–4" sprigs. Glue the longer sprigs behind the ammobium in the pot on the right and the shorter ones evenly spaced among the florals on the lower half of the wreath. Glue the sign at the wreath center top. Glue the tools below the pots as shown.

Oceanside Wreath

one 15" round grapevine
   wreath
25–30 assorted shells,
   1"–3" long
3 oz. of dried avena
2 oz. of blue dried lark-
   spur
2 oz. of dried tulyp star
2 yards of 2" wide cream
   seaside print wire-
   edged ribbon
22-gauge wire
low temperature glue
   gun and sticks

1 Attach a wire
hanger (see page
26) to the top back of
the wreath. Use the
ribbon to make an
oblong bow (see page
32) with a center loop,
two 3" loops, four 3½"
loops, two 6" tails, a
14" tail and an 18" tail.
Glue it to the wreath
at 11:00. Loop and glue the 18" tail to the right and the
14" tail down the left side.

2 Cut six 2"–3" sprigs of avena. Glue them among
the bow loops. Cut the rest of the avena into 4"–6"
sprigs. Glue a cluster of three sprigs behind each side of
the bow, angled as for the upper bow loops. Glue the
rest in clusters of 5–6 sprigs evenly spaced on both sides
of the bow tails, tucking the stems under the ribbon.
Choose two cone-shaped, similar shells and glue one to
extend from under each side of the bow. Glue two large
shells to each tail as shown.

3 Glue the remaining shells along the bow tails and
around the bow loops, varying the types and sizes.

4 Cut the larkspur into 4"–5" sprigs and the tulyp
star into 4"–6" sprigs. Glue a few sprigs on each
side of the bow and the rest evenly spaced among the
avena sprigs at similar angles.

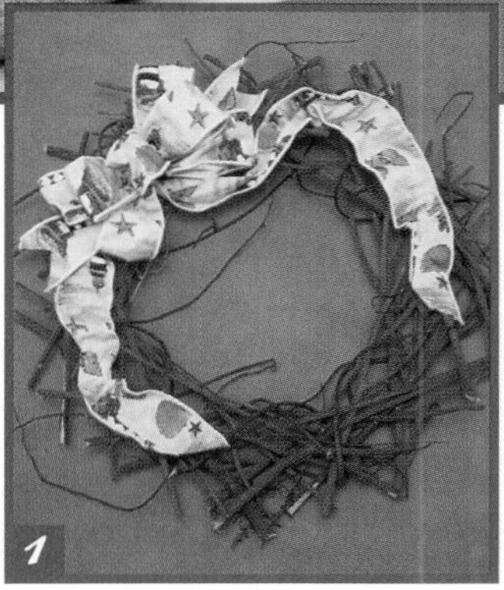

Ivy & Rose Wreath

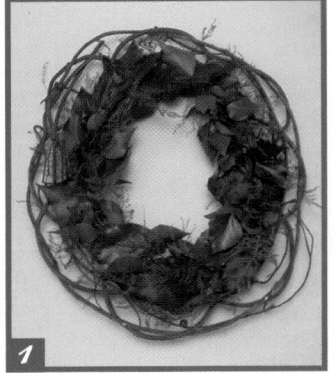

one 13"x16" TWIGS™ oval lace vine wreath
5 stems of 1" wide pink/yellow dried roses
2 oz. of green preserved ivy leaves
2 oz. of green preserved plumosus fern
2 oz. of dried caspia
2 oz. of pink dried pepperberries
3 oz. of white dried baby everlastings
2 oz. of dried Christina grass
1⅛ yards of 1½" wide golden yellow taffeta ribbon with pink wired edges
22-gauge wire, low temperature glue gun and sticks

1 Cut the ivy into 4" sprigs and glue them around the inner edge of the wreath, angled clockwise. Cut the plumosus into 4"–6" sprigs and glue them evenly spaced among the ivy sprigs.

2 Use the ribbon to make an oblong bow (see page 32) with a center loop, two 2½" loops, two 3" loops and 7" tails. Glue it to the center bottom of the greens. Cut the roses to 3" long and glue them evenly spaced around the wreath as shown.

3 Cut the caspia into 3"–4" sprigs and glue evenly spaced around the wreath, angled clockwise. Cut the pepperberries into 1"–2½" sprigs and glue as for the caspia.

4 Cut the baby everlastings into 1½"–3" sprigs and glue them evenly spaced throughout the design. Cut the Christina grass into 3"–4" sprigs and glue them evenly spaced among the flowers, angled clockwise.

Boxwood Floral Wreath

one 16" round grapevine wreath
8 stems of pink dried roses, 1" wide
4 oz. of green preserved eucalyptus
4 oz. of green preserved boxwood
3 oz. of green preserved plumosus fern
4 oz. of red dried pepperberries
4 oz. of lavender dried ti tree
3 oz. of white preserved rice flowers
2 oz. of dried bromus secalinus
3½ yards of 1½" wide violet organza wire-
    edged ribbon
22-gauge wire
low temperature glue gun and sticks

1 Attach a wire hanger (see page 26) to the top back of the wreath. Cut the eucalyptus into 5"–8" sprigs and glue them angled counterclockwise around the wreath. Repeat with the boxwood.

2 Cut the plumosus into 6"–10" sprigs and glue them evenly spaced among the eucalyptus and boxwood sprigs at similar angles, taking care to cover any bare areas of the wreath. Cut the roses to 6" long and glue them evenly spaced around the wreath, angling them alternately from inside to outside.

3 Cut the ti tree into 7" sprigs and glue them counterclockwise among the other florals, angling them alternately from inside to outside and slightly forward. Cut the pepperberries into 4"–6" sprigs and glue them evenly spaced among the roses and ti tree sprigs.

4 Cut the bromus and the rice flowers into 5"–8" sprigs and glue them evenly spaced around the wreath. Use the ribbon to make a puffy bow (see page 32) with a center loop, six 3½" loops and one 80" tail. Glue the bow at 4:00; tuck and glue the tail gently among the florals around the wreath as shown in the large photo.

Salal Wreath

one 14" round green pre-
 served salal wreath
5 stems of pink/yellow
 dried roses, ¾"–1"
 wide
2 oz. of green preserved
 austral fern
2 oz. of blue dried
 larkspur
2 oz. of pink dried
 larkspur
3 oz. of pink preserved
 rice flowers
2 oz. of white dried
 starflowers
2 oz. of blue dried caspia
3 yards of 1⅜" wide pink
 organza wire-edged
 ribbon
spray paints for florals:
 burgundy, copper
22-gauge wire
low temperature glue gun
 and sticks

1 Attach a wire hanger (see page 26) to the top back of the wreath. Lightly spray the wreath in three or four places with burgundy and copper spray paint, holding the spray can 12" away and moving it quickly to achieve an effect of depth, rather than overall color. Cut the fern into 5"–7" sprigs and glue them evenly spaced among the salal leaves.

2 Cut the blue larkspur into 4" and 8" sprigs. Glue the 8" sprigs around the outer edge of the wreath, evenly spaced and angled counterclockwise. Repeat to glue the 4" sprigs around the inside edge of the wreath. Cut the rice flowers into 4" sprigs and glue them throughout the salal. Cut the roses to 4" long and glue them evenly spaced around the wreath.

3 Cut the starflowers into 4" sprigs and wire them in clusters of 10–15 sprigs. Glue the clusters evenly spaced among the other florals. Cut the caspia into 5"–6" sprigs and glue them as for the starflower clusters, filling any sparse areas.

4 Cut the pink larkspur into 6" sprigs and the rice grass into 4"–7" sprigs; glue them evenly spaced throughout the design. Use the ribbon to make an oblong bow (see page 32) with a center loop, six 3" loops, four 5" loops, a 10" tail and a 15" tail. Glue the bow at 4:00 and drape the tails to the left, with the 10" tail above the 15" one; glue to secure.

Jeweled Garden Wreath

one 16" round grapevine wreath
seven 2" wide burgundy dried dahlia
 blossom heads
one 4" wide blossom head of yellow
 dried yarrow
6 oz. of white dried German statice
2 oz. of lavender dried suworowii statice
2 oz. of purple dried sinuata statice
4 oz. of green preserved eucalyptus
3 oz. of green preserved plumosus fern
2 oz. of burgundy preserved baby's
 breath
3¼ yards of 1½" wide purple taffeta
 wire-edged ribbon
22-gauge wire
low temperature glue gun and sticks

1 Attach a wire hanger (see page 26) to the top back of the wreath. Cut the German statice into 3"–5" sprigs and glue them around the wreath, angled counterclockwise, to completely cover it. Cut the eucalyptus into 6"–8" sprigs and glue them evenly spaced among the statice sprigs.

2 Cut the fern into 5"–8" sprigs and glue them among the statice and eucalyptus sprigs at similar angles. Glue the dahlias evenly spaced among the other materials, facing forward.

3 Cut the sinuata statice into 5"–7" sprigs and glue them evenly spaced along the inside and outside edges of the wreath. Cut the yarrow into eight 1" wide clusters and glue them 6" apart around the wreath, alternating between the inside and outside edges.

4 Cut the suworowii statice and the baby's breath into 7" sprigs and glue them evenly spaced around the wreath. Use the ribbon to make an oblong bow (see page 32) with a center loop, six 3" loops, four 5" loops, one 13" tail and one 21" tail. Glue it at 8:00 and drape the tails to the right as shown in the large photo; glue.

Wall Decor with Elegance & Style

There are many ways to decorate walls using dried flowers. Arches, crowns, garlands and swags are wonderful alternatives to the traditional wreath because of their variety of shape and the ability to use them when designing for unusual spaces.

The nature of arches, swags and garlands allows the designer to easily customize any piece to specific dimensions. A few additional sprigs of greenery or twigs added to the ends of a design can add length, while trimming the base material before adding florals provides the solution for small areas. The Raffia & Terra Cotta Braid (page 75) and Vertical Swag (page 73) were constructed on braided raffia and can be made longer or shorter simply by altering the braid length.

The Plumosus Garland (page 72) provides many design options as it can be hung horizontally over a window, curved over a mirror or hung in draped festoons to accent a wall over a bed. The Wreath Garland (page 70) can be reduced to three wreaths or made much longer by adding more wreaths; the supplies can be increased or decreased as needed. Because you are the designer, you can make the rules.

The Wall Basket (page 74) and the Wall Pocket (page 69) offer yet more options for floral wall decorations. While both are very pretty and would look wonderful on any wall, they are easily adaptable to become utilitarian as well.

The wide selection of pretty designs and the variety of styles on the following pages will spark imagination and provide many options for decorating your home.

8 oz. of green preserved willow eucalyptus
4 oz. of green preserved spiral eucalyptus
3 oz. of green preserved plumosus fern
3 oz. of pink preserved leptospermum
3 oz. of white preserved statice sinuata
3 oz. of lavender dried caspia
2 oz. of green preserved isolepsis grass

1 mauve silk rose stem with one 4" wide
  blossom
2 stems of mauve silk roses, each with a
  2" wide blossom
24-gauge wire
low temperature glue gun and sticks

Willow Eucalyptus

1   Divide the willow eucalyptus in half. Overlap the stems 4" and wire the two bunches
    together to form a 34" wide arch base. Cut the spiral eucalyptus into 4"–10" sprigs and glue
half on each side of the arch, extending toward the ends, with the shorter sprigs on the top and
the longer sprigs below them.

2   Cut the fern into 4"–10" sprigs and glue as for the spiral eucalyptus. Cut
    the stems off the silk roses and glue the large one to the arch center. Glue
a smaller rose 4" to each side of the large rose.

3   Cut the leptospermum into 6"–12" sprigs and glue evenly spaced among
    the fern, extending as for the spiral eucalyptus. Cut the sinuata statice into
4" sprigs and glue evenly spaced among the leptospermum.

4   Cut the caspia into 5"–8" sprigs and the isolepsis grass into 8"–12" sprigs.
    Glue them evenly spaced among the fern, extending outward. Attach a
wire hanger (see page 26) to the center back of the swag.

Victorian Swag

one 33"x14" TWIGS® Victorian swag
two 6" wide blue preserved hydrangea blossom heads
7 stems of pink dried roses, each 1" wide
4 oz. of green preserved leatherleaf fern
4 oz. of mauve preserved peppergrass
4 oz. of purple preserved lavender

3 oz. of white preserved sinuata statice
2 oz. of burgundy preserved rice flower
2¾ yards of 1¼" wide mauve sheer wire-edged ribbon
24-gauge wire
low temperature glue gun and sticks

1 Use the ribbon to make an oblong bow (see page 32) with a center loop, six 2½" loops, four 3½" loops and two 18" tails. Glue it to the lower arch center and extend a tail to each side, draping each through the twigs and gluing the ends to secure. Cut the fern into 4"–8" sprigs and glue evenly spaced on each side of the bow, extending toward the ends. Glue a few 4" sprigs above and below the bow, angled as shown.

2 Cut the peppergrass into 4"–6" sprigs and glue evenly spaced among the fern sprigs, extending in the same directions. Cut the lavender into 6"–7" sprigs and wire 4–6 together, making 14 clusters. Glue them evenly spaced among the other materials, extending as for the peppergrass.

3 Cut the hydrangea heads into 2"–4" wide sprigs; glue a few sprigs around the bow loops and the remaining sprigs evenly spaced among the other materials.

4 Cut the rice flower into 2"–3" sprigs and glue evenly spaced among the other materials. Cut the roses to 4". Glue them around the bow as shown in the large photo.

one 40" wide twig
    arch
one 9" grapevine
    wreath
five 4"–5" wide
    purple/tan dried
    hydrangea
    blossom heads
five 2"–3" whole
    dried oranges: 3
    green, 2 orange
four 2"–3"
    burgundy dried
    pomegranates
4 oz. of dried festuca
    grass
4 oz. of dried
    ambrosinia
3 oz. of dried avena
2 oz. (6 stems) of
    yellow dried
    yarrow
2 oz. of burgundy
    dried amaranthus
2 oz. of green dried
    hops
24-gauge wire
low temperature glue
    gun and sticks

Orange & Pomegranate Arch

1 Cut the festuca grass into 15" sprigs, then divide into six equal bunches. Wire each bunch together at the stem ends. Glue three bunches evenly spaced to each side of the arch, angled as shown by the yellow arrows. Divide the ambrosinia into five clusters. Cut one cluster into 6" sprigs. Wire each cluster together at the stem ends. Glue a long cluster between each festuca bunch (see the blue arrows). Glue the 6" cluster to the arch center, extending downward.

2 Glue one hydrangea head in the center of the arch and two evenly spaced on each side. Glue an orange to the left of each hydrangea, placing the colors as shown. Glue a pomegranate to the arch center, one on the left side and two on the right as shown.

3 Cut the yarrow into 3" sprigs and glue evenly spaced among the other materials. Cut the amaranthus into ten 5" sprigs and glue five evenly spaced to each side of the arch, angled as shown. Cut the hops into 5" sprigs and glue evenly and to fill empty areas.

4 Cut the avena into 6"–7" sprigs and glue evenly among the other materials. Undo the binding on the grapevine wreath and loosen the vines. Cut individual vines into 12"–14" sections. Glue the end of a vine at the right end of the arch, cross to the left side and glue the other end to secure. Continue gluing vines across the arch, positioning them as shown in the large photo. Attach a wire hanger (see page 26) to the center back of the arch.

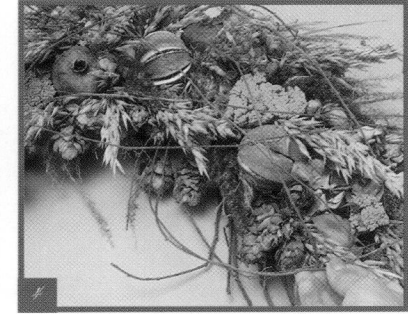

Wall Pocket

one 10"x15" oval wicker wall pocket
fifteen ⅜"–1¼" wide pink dried strawflowers
6 white dried strawflowers
one 3" pink dried cockscomb blossom
3 oz. of pink preserved heather
2 oz. of lavender dried pennyroyal
2 oz. of green preserved plumosus fern
2 oz. of white dried German statice
3⅓ yards of 1½" wide mauve taffeta ribbon
24-gauge wire
low temperature glue gun and sticks

1 Use the ribbon to make a puffy bow (see page 32) with a center loop, ten 3" loops, two 7" tails, one 15" tail and one 26" tail. Glue it to the basket at the right handle base. Angle the two short tails and the 15" tail downward, gluing to secure. Angle the 26" tail upward, over the basket handle, gluing to secure.

2 Cut the fern into 3"–6" sprigs. Glue 4–5 sprigs among the bow loops. Glue 8–10 sprigs 4" above the bow. Glue 4–5 sprigs on the left handle at 10:00 and 11:00. Glue the remaining sprigs at the base of the 26" tail, angling the sprigs as shown. Cut the German statice into 3"–5" sprigs and glue evenly spaced among each fern cluster, angling in the same directions.

3 Glue a white strawflower above and one below the bow. Glue one to the center of the fern sprigs above the bow. Glue two among the fern sprigs at the base of the 26" tail and one in the fern cluster directly above it. Glue three pink strawflowers evenly spaced among each fern cluster. Cut the cockscomb blossom into ½"–1" wide sprigs and glue among the strawflower clusters except the 11:00 cluster.

4 Cut the heather and pennyroyal into 3"–6" sprigs. Glue them evenly spaced in the clusters, extending downward on the lower left and lower right and extending upward elsewhere.

five 9" wide grapevine wreaths
4¼ yards of 1½" wide tan/white/cream
   taffeta wire-edged ribbon
14 stems of yellow dried roses, each 1" wide
2 oz. of dried club wheat

2 oz. of white dried larkspur
2 oz. of white preserved rice flower
2 oz. of dried festuca grass
24-gauge wire
low temperature glue gun and sticks

Wreath Garland

1 Wire the wreaths in an arc to make a garland. Cut two 15" lengths from the ribbon. Use each to make a standup bow (see page 33) with two 2" loops and one 5" tail. Glue one to the upper right end of the garland with the loops angled upward. Wrap the tail around the wreath and glue. Repeat with the other bow on the upper left end of the garland.

2 Cut the remaining ribbon into four 30" lengths. Tie one length over each wired area where two wreaths meet and finish each in a shoestring bow (see page 35) with two 2½" loops and two 6" tails. Cut eight roses to 3" and the stems off the rest. Glue two 3" roses above each shoestring bow as shown. Glue a stemless rose above each shoestring bow and at the base of each standup bow.

3 Cut a 2" wheat head and glue it behind the rose on a standup bow. Repeat for the other standup bow. Cut the remaining wheat into 3"–4" sprigs and set aside the stems. Glue three among each rose cluster, angling upward in the center and outward on each side. Cut the larkspur into 2"–5" sprigs; glue two short sprigs behind each standup bow and the remaining sprigs in the clusters as for the wheat. Cut leftover wheat stems into twenty 5" sprigs and glue five below each shoestring bow, extending downward.

4 Cut the rice flowers into 1"–2" sprigs and the festuca grass into 2"–6" sprigs. Glue evenly spaced among the four center floral clusters, extending as for the wheat. Attach a wire hanger (see page 26) to the middle and ends at the back of the swag.

Windowbox

one 14"x3"x4" white wood planter with a 15" tall window frame at the back
8 stems of red dried roses, each ¾"–1" wide
4 oz. of pink preserved leptospermum
3 oz. of purple dried caspia
2 oz. of green preserved ming fern
2 oz. of green preserved tree fern
2 oz. of white dried margaritas
2 oz. of blue dried lavender
2 oz. of yellow preserved leptospermum
1 oz. of green sphagnum moss
2¼ yards of ⅝" wide burgundy taffeta wire-edged ribbon
two 6"x2"x2" blocks of floral foam for drieds
24-gauge wire
low temperature glue gun and sticks

1 Cut the foam to fit inside the planter and cover with moss. Cut the ming fern into 5"–14" sprigs. Glue a 14" sprig into the back left of the planter, extending upward. Glue a 5" sprig 4½" from the right side of the planter, extending to the right and forward. Use the remaining fern to fill in the space between the 14" and 5" sprigs, with the shorter sprigs in front and the longer sprigs in back as shown. Angle a few sprigs to the left. Cut the tree fern into 5"–12" sprigs and repeat.

2 Cut the pink leptospermum into 4"–11" sprigs. Glue evenly spaced among fern sprigs of similar lengths, extending in similar directions. Cut one rose to 10", three to 7" and four to 4". Glue the 10" rose in front of the tallest fern sprigs. Glue the 7" roses in front of the 10" rose, all 2" apart. Glue two 4" roses among the far right ferns, a 4" rose into the front left corner with the remaining rose 2" to the right of it.

3 Cut the margaritas into 4"–10" sprigs and the lavender into 4"–12" sprigs. Glue both evenly spaced among other materials of similar lengths.

4 Cut the yellow leptospermum into 4"–12" sprigs and glue evenly spaced among the other materials, extending as for the pink leptospermum in step 2. Cut the caspia into 4"–12" sprigs and glue evenly, filling any empty areas. Use the ribbon to make a puffy bow (see page 32) with a center loop, eight 2½" loops, one 9" and one 19" tail. Glue the bow to the left front of the windowbox, just under the flowers. Angle and loop the tails to the right, gluing in several places to secure.

Plumosus Garland

six 4" wide blue preserved hydrangea blossom heads
6 oz. of green preserved plumosus fern
4 oz. of preserved baby's breath
4 oz. of mauve dried starflowers
4 oz. of burgundy dried hill flowers
3 oz. of pink dried strawflowers

4 yards of ¼" wide mauve satin ribbon
green floral tape
one 60" length of 22-gauge wire
24-gauge wire
low temperature glue gun and sticks

1 Hold the floral tape at a 45° angle against one end of the 60" wire. Begin wrapping the tape around the wire, keeping it at an angle. Stretch the tape as you wrap (this makes it stick to itself). Wrap the wire completely. Bend each wire end into a hanging loop, as shown in the lower photo. Attach another hanger in the center.

2 Cut the plumosus into 6"–8" sprigs, the baby's breath into 5" sprigs and the starflowers and hill-flowers into 4" sprigs. Make a small bouquet with 4–5 plumosus sprigs as the base, two baby's breath sprigs on top, five hill flowers on the right and 15 starflowers on the left. Wire the bouquet together at the bottom. Make 11 more bouquets, then make 12 bouquets with the starflowers and hill flowers reversed.

3 Begin constructing the garland by wiring a bouquet to the left end of the taped wire with the flowers extending beyond the end of the wire. Without cutting the binding wire, add a second cluster below the first and wire to secure. Alternate the bouquets so the starflowers extend both right and left along the garland. Repeat to the end of the wrapped wire.

4 Cut the hydrangea heads into 2" wide sprigs. Glue the hydrangea sprigs and strawflower blossoms evenly spaced to the garland, alternately extending upward and downward. Cut the ribbon into three 38" and three 10" lengths. Use each 38" length to make a loopy bow (see page 33) with a center loop, six 2" loops and two 5" tails. Tie each bow with the 10" length, creating another set of tails. Glue one bow to the center of the garland and one at each end.

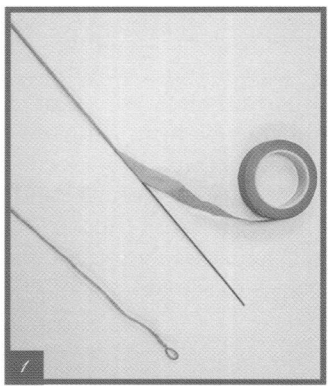

Vertical Swag

10 stems of pink dried roses, each ½" wide
3¼ yards of 1½" wide dark purple taffeta wire-edged ribbon
three 4" wide blue preserved hydrangea blossom heads
one 34" long green braided raffia swag (if one is unavailable, buy
   3 oz. of 36" long green raffia and braid one)
3 oz. of purple dried ti tree
2 oz. of green dried German statice
2 oz. of purple preserved sinuata statice
2 oz. of pink dried starflowers
2 oz. of purple preserved lavender
2 oz.of dark green preserved austral fern
24-gauge wire
1 U-shaped floral pin
low temperature glue gun and sticks

1 Cut the German statice and fern into 3"–4" sprigs and
glue them evenly spaced down the raffia swag, extending
the sprigs at the top upward and the rest downward.

2 Cut the roses to 3" and glue them evenly spaced down
the swag front angled as shown. Cut the ti tree into 4"–5"
sprigs and glue evenly spaced among the roses, extending as
for the German statice.

3 Cut the hydrangea into 2"–3" sprigs and glue evenly
among the other materials. Use the ribbon to make a
puffy bow (see page 33) with a center loop, eight 3" loops and
30" tails. Glue it 3" below the swag top, with a tail extending
down each side of the swag. Glue in several places to secure.

4 Cut the sinuata statice into 3" sprigs and glue evenly
among the other materials, extending as for the German
statice. Cut the starflowers into 4" sprigs. Glue 12 sprigs among
the bow loops and the rest in clusters of 6–8, with a few individual sprigs among the bow loops. Cut the lavender into 5" sprigs
and glue as for the statice. Use a U-pin to make a hanger (see
page 26) and glue to the upper swag back.

one 12"x16" TWIGS® wall basket
4 oz. of green preserved needle grass
3 oz. of brown preserved lecchio
3 stems of yellow dried yarrow
3 oz. of green sphagnum moss
2 oz. of light green dried ambrosinia

2 oz. of dried nigella orientalis
2 oz. of purple dried oregano
2 oz. of dried rice grass
2 oz. of 48" long raffia
24-gauge wire
low temperature glue gun and sticks

1 Cut the needle grass into 5"–8" sprigs. Glue the longer sprigs to the outside of the basket on the left side, extending upward, and the remaining sprigs on the sides and bottom, extending as shown. Cut the ambrosinia into 4"–7" sprigs and glue evenly spaced among the needle grass, extending in the same manner.

2 Cut the lecchio into 3"–7" sprigs and glue near materials of similar lengths, extending in the same directions. Cut the yarrow into a 2" wide sprig and two 3" wide sprigs. Glue the 2" sprig in the lower left. Glue the 3" sprigs as shown.

3 Cut the nigella orientalis into 3"–5" sprigs and glue evenly spaced among the other materials, extending as for lecchio. Cut the oregano into 3"–6" sprigs and glue evenly spaced among the other materials to fill any empty areas.

4 Use the raffia to make a collar bow (see page 34) with two 3" loops and 18" tails. Glue the bow above the 2" yarrow sprig and angle the tails to the right, gluing in many places to secure. Cut the rice grass into 4" sprigs and glue evenly spaced among the other materials, extending in similar directions. Fill the basket with moss, tucking moss tufts to fill the empty areas.

Raffia & Terra Cotta Braid

one 32" long braided raffia swag (if one
   is unavailable, buy 3 oz. of 36" long
   raffia and braid one)
three 2½" wide terra cotta pots
2 oz. of dried avena
2 oz. of purple dried lavender
2 oz. of green preserved lepidium
2 oz. of pink preserved genista
2 oz. of yellow dried mini
   chrysanthemums
2 oz. of dried nigella
1 oz. of green sphagnum moss
1 oz. of 30" long raffia
one 6"x2"x2" block of floral foam for
   drieds
serrated knife
24-gauge wire
1 U-shaped floral pin
low temperature glue gun and sticks

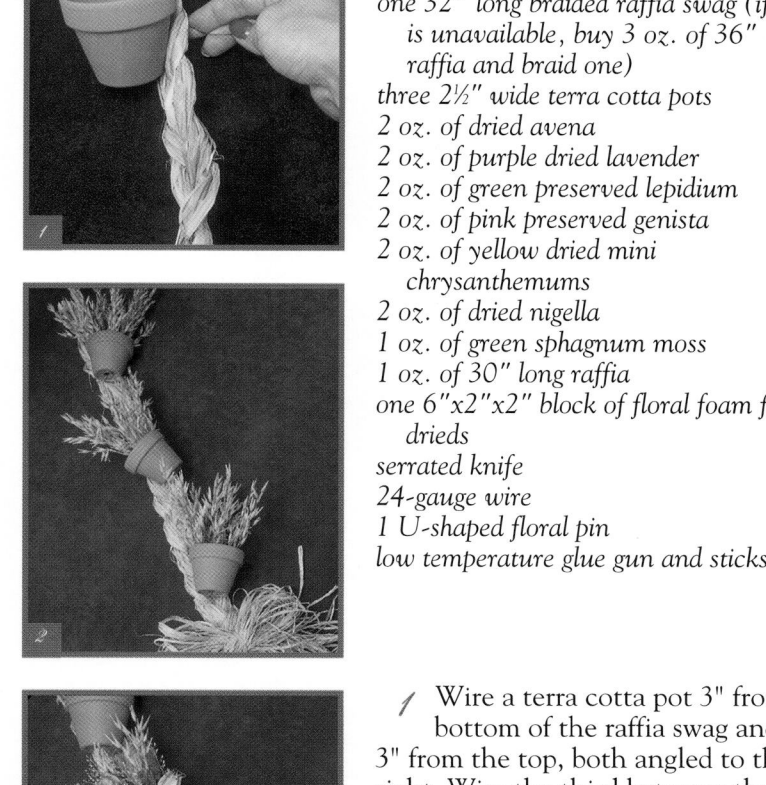

1   Wire a terra cotta pot 3" from the
    bottom of the raffia swag and one
3" from the top, both angled to the
right. Wire the third between them,
extending to the left. Glue each pot to
the braid for added reinforcement.

2   Set aside twelve raffia strands and use the rest to make a collar bow (see page
    34) with two 3½" loops and 4" tails. Glue it over the wire at the bottom of the
braid. Cut the foam into three 2" squares; glue a square into each pot and cover each
with moss. Cut the avena into 3"–6" sprigs and divide into three clusters. Glue each
cluster into a pot, extending in the same direction the pot is tilted.

3   Cut the lavender and the lepidium into 3"–6" sprigs. Set aside a few sprigs of each
    for step 4 and glue the rest evenly spaced among the avena. Cut the nigella into
3"–4" sprigs. Glue four into the top and bottom pot and three into the middle pot.

4   Cut the genista into 3"–7" sprigs and glue a few sprigs to the bow center, extend-
    ing outward. Glue the remaining sprigs evenly spaced in each pot, extending as
for the other materials. Cut the chrysanthemums into 2"–5" sprigs. Glue two sprigs in
the bow center and the rest evenly as for the genista. Glue the saved lavender and lepidium to the bow center, extending outward. Use four strands of the remaining raffia
to tie each pot to the braid finishing in a shoestring bow (see page 35) with two 1"
loops and 2" tails. Use a floral U-pin to make a hanger (see page 26) and glue to the
upper swag back.

one 28" wide green preserved spiral
   eucalyptus swag
4 oz. of 3" long red dried chili peppers
   on stems
3 oz. of dried barley
3 oz. of dried ambrosinia
3 oz. of yellow preserved leptospermum

2 oz. of green dried hops
2 oz. of green dried linum
2 yards of sea grass rope
two 1¾" wide rope-covered balls
24-gauge wire
low temperature glue gun and sticks

1 Cut the barley into 4"–9" sprigs. Glue half on each side of the swag, extending as for the eucalyptus, with the shorter sprigs toward the center. Cut the ambrosinia into 5"–8" sprigs and glue as for the barley.

2 Cut a 7" section of rope and set aside. Use the rest to make a loopy bow (see page 33) with two 3" loops, four 4" loops and 9" tails. Glue it to the swag center. Glue a rope ball to the end of each tail by cutting ¼" of rope off the end of the ball, filling the hole with glue, then holding the tail end firmly in the glue until it sets. Coil the 7" section of sea grass in the bow center as shown and glue to secure.

3 Cut the chili peppers into 3"–7" sprigs. Glue the shorter sprigs among the bow loops and the longer sprigs into the swag, all sprigs extending toward the ends. Cut the leptospermum into 4"–7" sprigs and glue near the chili peppers of similar lengths.

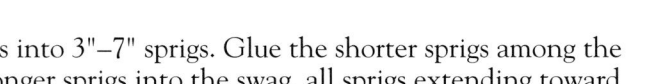

4 Cut the hops into 4" sprigs and the linum into 6"–9" sprigs. Glue both evenly spaced among the other materials, extending toward the swag ends. Attach a wire hanger (see page 26) to the center back of the swag.

Wheat Sheaf

4 oz. of dried black-bearded wheat
2 oz. of rust preserved oak leaves
2 oz. of orange/green dried safflower
2 oz. of yellow dried solidago
2 oz. of orange preserved leptospermum
2 oz. of brown dried cattails
2 oz. of blue preserved erica mediterranea
2 oz. of 45" long raffia
dried pomegranates: one 1¾" wide, one 2¼" wide
24-gauge wire
low temperature glue gun and sticks

1 Hold the wheat together under the heads and wire the bunch together. Use the wire ends to make a hanger (see page 26) at the back. Fan the bunch by pulling the wheat in the back upward and the outer stems to each side. The longest sprigs should extend 14" above the wire. Use the raffia to make a raffia collar bow (see page 34) with two 3" loops and 18" tails. Glue to the wheat sheaf over the wire.

2 Cut the oak leaves into 4"–6" sprigs and glue them to the wheat sheaf angled from the upper left to the lower right as shown. Glue the pomegranates over the bow center, with the smaller extending to the upper right and the larger to the lower left.

3 Cut the safflower into three 3" and two 4½" sprigs. Glue a sprig of each size under the lower pomegranate, extending downward, and above the upper pomegranate, angling to the upper right. Glue a 3" sprig to the left of the upper pomegranate, angled upward. Cut the solidago into 2"–4" sprigs and glue around the pomegranates, angling as for the safflower sprigs.

4 Cut the leptospermum into 4"–6" sprigs and glue evenly spaced around the pomegranates, extending outward. Cut the cattails into 5"–10" sprigs. Glue the longer sprigs above the pomegranates and the shorter sprigs to the sides, angled as shown. Cut the erica into 3"–6" sprigs and glue evenly among the other materials.

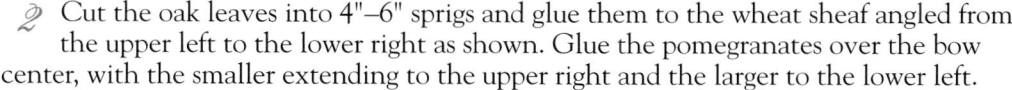
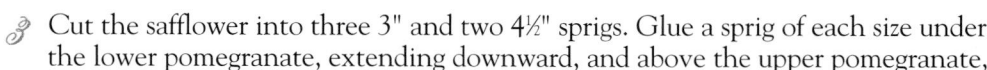
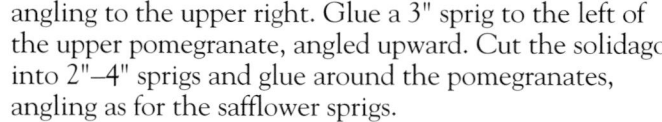
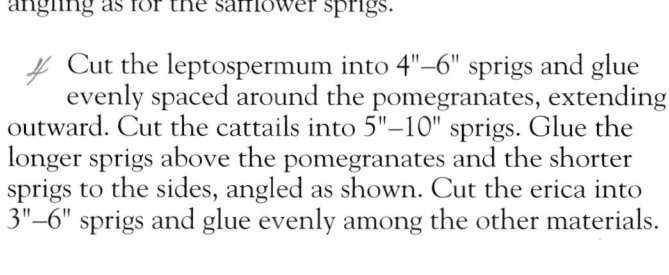

one 18″ long green preserved salal arch
two 3″ wide yellow dried yarrow blossoms
3 oz. of dried barley
3 oz. of purple dried pennyroyal
3 oz. of green preserved dudinea
3 oz. of red preserved spiral eucalyptus
2 oz. of green preserved hops
2½ yards of 2½″ wide tan/red gingham wire-edged ribbon
24-gauge wire
low temperature glue gun and sticks

3 Cut the pennyroyal into 5″–6″ sprigs. Cut three 6″ sprigs in half and glue among the bow loops. Glue the remaining sprigs evenly among the other materials in clusters of 5–6, extending downward. Cut the dudinea into 3″–4″ sprigs. Glue a few 3″ sprigs among the bow loops, extending outward, and one sprig above the bow, extending upward. Glue the remaining sprigs evenly to fill the swag, extending downward.

4 Cut four 3″ sprigs of eucalyptus and glue among the bow loops, extending outward and upward. Cut the remaining eucalyptus into 4″–6″ sprigs and glue evenly spaced among the other materials, extending downward. Cut the yarrow blossoms into ½″–¾″ wide sprigs and glue evenly spaced among the salal and bow. Attach a wire hanger (see page 26) to the upper swag back.

1 Straighten the wire support to form a straight 22″ long swag. Use the ribbon to make an oblong bow (see page 32) with a center loop, two 2″ loops, four 3″ loops, two 4″ loops and 18″ tails. Glue it over the stem ends at the top. Extend a tail down each side of the arch, gluing every 4″.

2 Cut the barley into 4″ sprigs and glue in clusters of 3–5 sprigs evenly among the salal, extending downward. Cut the hops into 3″–5″ sprigs and glue evenly spaced among the salal leaves.

Nature's Swag

one 34" long TWIGS® swag
three 2"–3" dried pomegranates
three 2"–3" brown dried lotus pods
3 oz. of green dried bay leaves
3 oz. of burgundy preserved amaranthus
2 oz. of green preserved spiral eucalyptus
2 oz. of dried nigella

2 oz. of brown dried rice grass
2 oz. of brown preserved lecchio
3¼ yards of 1½" wide brown/tan ombré wire-edged ribbon
24-gauge wire
low temperature glue gun and sticks

3 Use the ribbon to make an oblong bow (see page 32) with a center loop, two 3½" loops, two 4" loops, two 4½" loops, two 15" tails and two 17" tails. Glue it to the swag center and weave a tail of each length among the materials on each side. Glue a lotus pod just under the bow, one 6" to the left and one 5" to the right of the center pod.

1 Cut the eucalyptus into 4"–12" sprigs. Glue to the swag center, extending toward each end, with the longer sprigs on the bottom, near the ends, and the shorter sprigs on the top, near the center. Cut the bay into 7"–9" sprigs and cut the leaves off 10 sprigs. Glue the sprigs among the eucalyptus sprigs, extending in the same direction. Glue the individual leaves to the swag center, angling as shown.

2 Cut the amaranthus into 6"–9" sprigs and glue evenly spaced near materials of similar lengths, extending in the same directions. Glue a pomegranate to the swag center, angling left, one 5" to the left and one 5" to the right of the center pomegranate.

4 Cut the nigella into 4"–6" sprigs and glue individually or in pairs among the other materials, extending in the same directions. Cut the lecchio into 5"–9" sprigs and glue evenly extending outward from the bow loops. Cut the rice grass into 4"–7" sprigs and glue among the bay, extending in the same directions. Cut a few twigs from the back of the swag and glue on each side of the bow, extending outward. Attach a wire hanger (see page 26) to the center back of the swag.

Rose & Salal Arch

1 Cut the salal into 4"–6" sprigs. Glue the sprigs to cover the arch, extending as shown. Glue the shortest sprigs in the center, angling upward and downward.

2 Cut the fern into 3"–6" sprigs and glue evenly spaced among the salal. Cut the roses to 3" and glue one to the arch center. Evenly glue five roses to each side of the arch, alternating between the top and bottom edge. Cut the pepperberries into 3"–6" sprigs and glue evenly among the other materials, extending as for the salal.

3 Cut the heather into 5"–7" sprigs and glue as for the pepperberries, following the curve of the arch.

4 Cut the hydrangea heads into 2"–3" wide sprigs and glue evenly among the other materials. Cut the sinuata into 3" sprigs and the larkspur into 4"–5". Glue both as for the pepperberries. Attach a wire hanger (see page 26) to the center back of the arch.

one 18" grapevine arch
11 dark pink dried roses, each ¾" wide
3 oz. of blue preserved heather
3 oz. of white preserved sinuata statice
3 oz. of white dried larkspur
2 oz. of red dried preserved pepperberries
2 oz. of green preserved austral fern
two 4"–5" wide blue preserved hydrangea blossom heads
24-gauge wire
low temperature glue gun and sticks

Corner Swag

one 14"x17" TWIGS® corner
  swag
one 4" wide blue preserved
  hydrangea blossom head
3 oz. of green preserved
  plumosus
3 oz. of dark pink preserved
  leptospermum
3 oz. of purple preserved
  sinuata statice
2 oz. of white dried caspia
2 oz. of burgundy preserved
  rice flowers
2¼ yards of 1½" wide mauve
  taffeta ribbon
24-gauge wire
low temperature glue gun and
  sticks

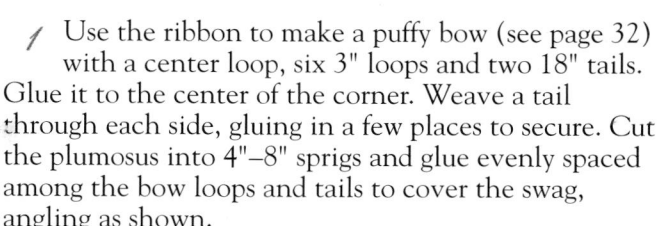

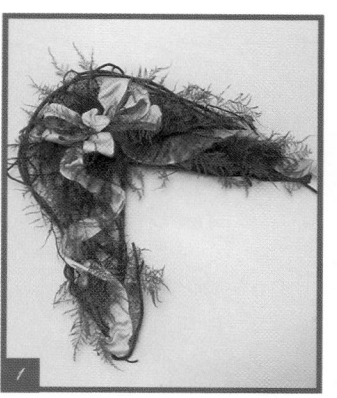

1. Use the ribbon to make a puffy bow (see page 32) with a center loop, six 3" loops and two 18" tails. Glue it to the center of the corner. Weave a tail through each side, gluing in a few places to secure. Cut the plumosus into 4"–8" sprigs and glue evenly spaced among the bow loops and tails to cover the swag, angling as shown.

2. Cut the leptospermum into 3"–6" sprigs. Glue the shorter sprigs among the bow loops. Glue the longer sprigs evenly spaced, extending toward each end of the swag.

3. Cut the statice and hydrangea into 2"–3" sprigs and glue evenly among the other materials.

4. Cut the caspia into 3"–4" sprigs and the rice flowers into 2" sprigs. Glue evenly among the other materials, angling as for the leptospermum. Attach a wire hanger (see page 26) to the center back corner.

Bird's Ladder

14"x25" TWIGS® ladder
11 stems of pink dried roses, each ¾" wide
3 oz. of green preserved plumosus fern
2 oz. of blue dried caspia
2 oz. of purple preserved lavender
2 oz. of white dried sinuata statice
2 yards of 1½" wide mauve taffeta wire-edged ribbon
mauve mushroom birds: two 3", one 2", four 1"
3 nest picks, each with a 3" nest and a 6" twig spray
three ½" brown speckled plastic eggs
24-gauge wire
low temperature glue gun and sticks

1 Glue a nest at the top left, one at the bottom left and the last at the right on the second rung. Cut the fern into 3"–7" sprigs. Glue a cluster of sprigs at the top left and a cluster to the second rung on the right. Glue another cluster on the third rung at the left. Glue sprigs on the bottom rung evenly across the entire rung with a few sprigs tucked behind the nest. Cut the roses to 2" and glue 1–3 among each fern cluster as shown.

2 Cut the caspia into 3"–7" sprigs and the lavender into 3"–4" sprigs. Glue them evenly spaced to each fern cluster, extending as for the fern. Cut the sinuata into ½"–1" sprigs and glue evenly spaced around the roses.

3 Glue a 3" bird into the nest on the second rung and another on the third rung fern cluster. Glue a 1" bird on the third rung at the right, two into the nest at the ladder top and one on the twigs extending from the top nest. Glue a 2" bird in the center of the bottom rung.

4 Glue one end of the ribbon at the lower right with a 6" tail extending to the left. Loop the long end of the ribbon gently through the ladder rungs from side to side as shown, working to the top. Glue the end of the ribbon behind the upper left nest with a 4" tail extending downward to the right as shown in the large photo. Glue the eggs in the nest on the bottom left.

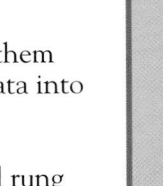

Garden Arbor

one 24"x11" TWIGS® fence with a
  center arch
one 10"x6" TWIGS® gate
three 4" wide pink preserved hydrangea
  blossom heads
3 oz. of light blue dried larkspur
3 oz. of pink dried ixodia daisies
2 oz. of light green preserved peppergrass

2 oz. of yellow preserved genista
2 oz. of white dried ammobium
2 oz. of green sphagnum moss
2 oz. of green preserved austral fern
flat white spray paint
24-gauge wire
low temperature glue gun and sticks

1   Spray the gate and arch lightly with the white paint; let dry. Glue the moss across the bottom rung of the fence. Wire the gate to the arch center.

2   Cut the fern into 3"–5" sprigs. Glue around the end fence posts, gate and arch as shown. Cut the hydrangea head into 2"–3" wide sprigs and glue evenly spaced among the moss, with some sprigs extending from behind the fence. Cut the larkspur into 3"–6" sprigs and glue among the fern sprigs, extending in the same direction.

3   Cut the genista into 3"–6" sprigs and the ammobium into 3" sprigs. Glue both evenly among the other materials, extending as for the larkspur, with the ammobium in clusters of 2–3 sprigs.

4   Cut the peppergrass into 3"–5" sprigs and the ixodia daisies into 2"–3" sprigs. Glue evenly spaced among the other sprigs.

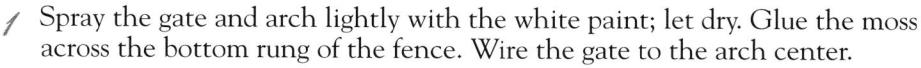

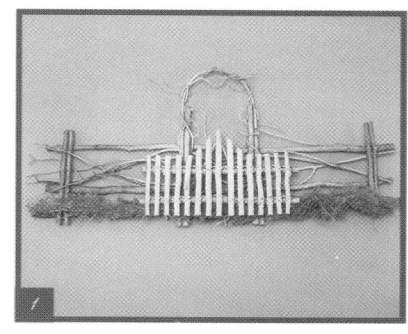

one 22"x14" TWIGS® fan
5 stems of yellow dried yarrow
two 3"–4" wide dark pink dried
 cockscomb blossoms
3 oz. of dried wheat
3 oz. of pink preserved genista
3 oz. of green preserved peppergrass
3 oz. of purple preserved statice
3 oz. of yellow preserved leptospermum
2 oz. of white dried larkspur
2 oz. of gray dried caspia
1 oz. of green sphagnum moss
1½ yards of 1½" wide green taffeta
 wire-edged ribbon
one 4"x2"x2" block of floral foam for
 drieds
24-gauge wire
low temperature glue gun and sticks

Floral Fan

1 Glue the foam to the lower fan front, above the base. Glue the moss below the
 foam. Cut the wheat into six 10" and seven 6" sprigs. Glue a 6" sprig into each
side of the foam, extending parallel to the base. Insert the 10" sprigs across the back
of the foam, forming a fan shape. Insert the remaining 6" sprigs in front of the 10"
sprigs, forming another fan. Cut the genista into 6"–11" sprigs and insert them among
the wheat sprigs of a similar lengths.

2 Cut the peppergrass into 6"–10" sprigs and insert them near materials of similar
 lengths, extending as for the wheat. Insert the shorter sprigs into the foam front.
Cut the caspia into 4"–10" sprigs and insert into the foam as for the peppergrass.

3 Cut the statice into 4"–10" sprigs and insert evenly near materials of similar
 lengths. Cut the cockscomb blossoms into 2" wide sprigs and glue evenly spaced
throughout the lower design front. Cut the yarrow into a 9", two 7" and two 4" sprigs
and insert as shown.

4 Cut the leptospermum and larkspur into 4"–10"
 sprigs and insert as for the peppergrass. Use the
ribbon to make an oblong bow (see page 32) with a
center loop, two 2" loops, two 2½" loops, two 3" loops
and two 7" tails. Do not fluff the loops and glue it to the
lower fan front, over the moss, and arrange a tail to
each side. Attach a wire hanger (see page 26) to the
upper fan back.

Regal Rose Arch

one 22" wide green preserved salal arch
5 stems of red dried Tivoli roses, each 3"
  wide
4 oz. of purple preserved leptospermum
3 oz. of blue preserved misty limonium
3 oz. of white preserved rice flower

3 oz. of green preserved plumosus
3 oz. of red preserved peppergrass
2¼ yards of 2" wide black/gold metallic
  wire-edged ribbon
24-gauge wire
low temperature glue gun and sticks

1 Use the ribbon to make an oblong bow (see page 32) with a center loop, two 3" loops, four 2½" loops and two 22" tails. Glue the bow to the right end of the arch. Loop and glue the tails over and under the arch as shown.

2 Cut the stems of the roses to 1". Glue a rose above and right of the bow and one to the left end. Glue the other three roses as shown.

3 Cut the limonium into 3"–6" sprigs and the rice flower into 2"–3" sprigs. Glue both evenly spaced among the other materials, angling to the left.

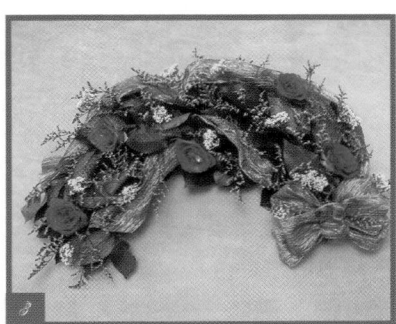

4 Cut the leptospermum and the plumosus into 4"–7" sprigs and the peppergrass into 3"–6" sprigs. Glue all evenly spaced among the other materials, angling to the left. Attach a wire hanger (see page 26) to the center back of the arch.

Center of Attention

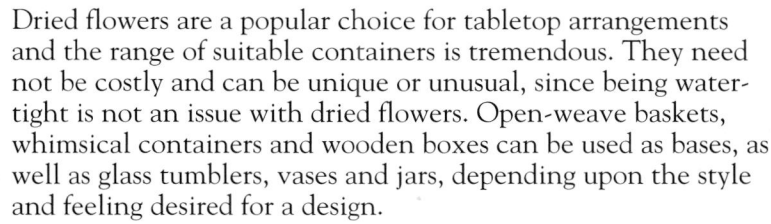

Dried flowers are a popular choice for tabletop arrangements and the range of suitable containers is tremendous. They need not be costly and can be unique or unusual, since being watertight is not an issue with dried flowers. Open-weave baskets, whimsical containers and wooden boxes can be used as bases, as well as glass tumblers, vases and jars, depending upon the style and feeling desired for a design.

The type of container you choose will play a large part in developing the theme for your arrangement. Wood boxes and woven baskets make a great complement to grains and grasses, while ceramics dress up a garden composition, and tin or copper kitchenware can lend a country look to an arrangement.

The Larkspur Birdhouse (page 97) and Garden Rocker (page 95) both feature whimsical bases on which to construct arrangements. Flowers can also be applied to the surface of a container rather than inside it, such as the Devonshire Garden Basket (page 96). The design therefore can be utilitarian as well as a beautiful addition to home decor.

When choosing a design, keep in mind the table it will sit on and the height that is best for that area. Constantly moving an arrangement to talk around it or to go about daily activities can be avoided by creating a lower or smaller design. Consider also that an arrangement sitting on a dining table will be viewed from all sides and should be attractive and full from any angle.

The designs included in this section provide many possibilities for creating the perfect arrangement for any space in the home—and the perfect arrangement can add polish, definition as well as a finishing touch to a room's decor.

Basket Bouquet

one 9"x12"x3" white wicker
    gathering basket with a 6" tall
    handle
8 stems of red dried roses, each 1½"
    wide
4 oz. of green preserved austral fern
3 oz. of white preserved ti tree
2 oz. of purple dried caspia
2 oz. of white preserved rice flower
2 oz. of red dried pepperberries
1 oz. of green sphagnum moss
1¾ yards of 1½" wide purple satin
    wire-edged ribbon
one 4"x3"x2" block of floral foam
    for drieds
24-gauge wire
low temperature glue gun and sticks

1 Glue the foam into the basket center. Cover the foam with the moss. Cut the fern fronds off the stems and into 4"–8" sprigs. Glue the longest sprigs into the right end of the foam, extending over the edge of the basket; glue the shorter sprigs around the edges and over the top of the foam. Cut the fern stems to 5" and insert in a cluster into the left of the foam, extending over the basket edge.

2 Cut two roses to 4" and six to 6". Insert the 4" roses into the left end of the foam, extending upward. Glue the remaining roses evenly spaced among the ferns, extending as shown. Cut the ti tree into 4"–8" sprigs and glue evenly spaced among the other materials, extending as for the fern.

3 Cut the caspia into 4"–6" and the rice flowers into 3" sprigs. Glue all the sprigs evenly spaced into the foam, extending as for the other materials.

4 Cut the pepperberries into 2"–4" sprigs and glue evenly spaced into the foam, extending as for the other materials. Use the ribbon to make an oblong bow (see page 32) with a center loop, two 2½" loops, four 3½" loops and two 6" tails. Glue to left side of the basket over the fern stems as shown.

Flower Cart

one 6½"x10"x5½" wood cart with a 7" long
    handle
terra cotta pots: one 2" wide, two 2½" wide
one 2" wide terra cotta saucer
one 3" tall tin watering can
one 3"x5" stuffed cloth seed packet
two 3" long wood/tin garden tools
four 2"–4" wide blue preserved hydrangea
    blossom heads
2 oz. of purple preserved rice flower
2 oz. of fuschia preserved sinuata statice
2 oz. of mauve dried starflowers
2 oz. of green preserved plumosus fern
2 oz. of white dried ammobium
2 oz. of blue preserved leptospermum
2 oz. of pink preserved misty limonium
2 oz. of green mood moss
floral foam for drieds: one 9"x5"x2" block,
    three 2"x2" blocks
24-gauge wire
low temperature glue gun and sticks

1   Glue the large piece of foam into the cart. Glue the seed packet to the
    back left corner of the design. Glue a 2½" pot to the front left, angled
toward the cart handle. Glue the 2" saucer on its side just right of the seed
packet. Glue the remaining 2½" pot to the right of the saucer, sitting upright
Glue the watering can to the center front of the design. Glue a 2" pot in the
front right corner of the design, angled forward.

2   Cover the exposed foam with moss. Trim the 2"x2" pieces of foam to fit
    into the pots and glue to secure. Insert a garden tool into the foam at the
front left and back right, angled as shown. Cut the rice flower and statice into
3" sprigs and insert into the back 2½" pot.

3   Cut the starflowers into 3" sprigs, wire together and glue into the foam
    front between the watering can and the right 2½" wide pot. Cut the fern
into 4"–7" sprigs and glue evenly spaced throughout the design. Glue a 2" wide
hydrangea head into the watering can. Glue a 4" wide blossom into the front
left corner, angled outward. Glue the remaining blossoms into the center of the
right and left ends.

4   Cut the ammobium into 3" sprigs and
    glue half into the front left pot. Divide
the remainder in half and glue half into the
back center of the cart and half into the front
right pot. Cut the leptospermum and the
misty limonium into 4"–7" sprigs and glue
evenly spaced throughout the design, with
the longer sprigs to the outside and the shorter sprigs in the center.

Boxed Treasure

one 11"x6½"x6½" papier-
    maché box with a dome lid
terra-cotta-colored spray paint
1⅔ yards of 1½" wide bur-
    gundy/pink ombré wire-
    edged ribbon
13 stems of pink dried roses,
    each 1½" wide
3 oz. of green dried bloom
    broom
2 oz. of purple/tan dried nigella
2 oz. of white dried larkspur
2 oz. of pink preserved mini
    baby's breath
2 oz. of burgundy dried brisa
    maxima
one 9"x3"x6" block of floral
    foam for drieds
24-gauge wire
low temperature glue gun and
    sticks

1 Gently remove the lid from the box and spray both with the paint; let dry. Glue the foam in the bottom center of the box. Cut seven roses to 5" and six to 3". Glue a cluster of three 6" roses in each front corner of the
foam, extending over the box edge. Glue a cluster of three 5" roses into the foam center with a cluster of two 5"
roses on each side as shown.

2 Cut the nigella into 4" sprigs and glue in clusters of 2 or 3, evenly spaced across the top of the foam. Cut the
bloom broom into 4"–6" sprigs and glue among the other materials.

3 Cut the larkspur into 3"–5"
sprigs. Glue them evenly spaced
among the other materials with the
longer sprigs extending upward
among the center sprigs and the
shorter one extending outward along
the front and sides. Cut the baby's
breath into 4"–6" sprigs and repeat.

4 Cut the brisa into 4" sprigs and
glue evenly spaced among the
other materials. Cut a 36" length of
ribbon and wrap it centered around
the box, gluing the ends in the front
to secure. Use the rest of the ribbon
to make a Dior bow (see page 35)
with a center loop, two 3" loops and
two 4" tails. Glue it over the ribbon
ends. Glue the box top to the back of
the box extending forward, as shown.

Watering Can

one 10"x12" wide tin watering can with a
   10" long spout
6 oz. of dried papaver
4 oz. of yellow dried solidago
3 oz. of dried bromus grass
3 oz. of pink dried larkspur
3 oz. of blue dried larkspur
3 oz. of dried festuca grass
3 oz. of dried lagurus
2 oz. of raffia, 40" long
four 9"x5"x4" blocks of floral foam for
   drieds, serrated knife
24-gauge wire
low temperature glue gun and sticks

1   Glue three blocks of foam on end
    into the watering can. Cut the
remaining foam in half and glue one half
centered on top of the other blocks; save
the remaining piece for another project.
Cut the bromus into three 16" sprigs,
seventeen 10" sprigs and twenty 13"–15"
sprigs. Glue the 16" sprigs into the center of the foam, extending upward. Glue
the 10" sprigs around the rim, extending
outward. Glue the 13"–15" sprigs evenly
spaced between the 16" and 10" sprigs,
extending as shown.

2   Cut the pink larkspur into 10"–16" sprigs and glue
    evenly spaced near bromus of similar lengths. Cut
eight 7" and eight 15" sprigs of blue larkspur. Glue the
7" sprigs evenly spaced around the rim, extending outward. Insert one 15" sprig in the center, extending
upward. Insert the remaining 15" sprigs evenly spaced
around the center 15" sprig. Cut the remaining blue
larkspur into 12" sprigs and insert between the 7" and
15" sprigs, extending outward, maintaining the rounded
shape of the arrangement.

3   Cut half of the solidago into 10" sprigs and half into
    15" sprigs. Insert the 10" sprigs among the outer
sprigs. Insert the 15" sprigs among the center sprigs. Cut
the papaver into 10"–16" sprigs and glue in clusters of
three evenly spaced near materials of similar lengths.

4   Cut the festuca grass into 10"–18" sprigs and glue
    into the foam with the longer sprigs near the cen-
ter, extending upward, and the shorter sprigs around the
outside, extending outward. Cut the lagurus into
10"–15" sprigs and repeat. Use the raffia to make a collar bow (see page 34) with 4" loops and 9" tails. Glue to
the front of the watering can.

one 14"x7"x5½" kidney-shaped
   willow basket
6 oz. of purple preserved lavender
6 oz. of sage green stemmed bay
   leaves
6 oz. of pink preserved heather
4 oz. of white dried ixodia daisy
4 oz. of sage green dried ambrosinia
4 oz. of green preserved plumosus
   fern
3 oz. of dried achillia verticor
eleven 2"–4" wide blue preserved
   hydrangea blossom heads
6 stems of pink freeze-dried
   snapdragons
5 stems of pink preserved roses, each
   1"–2" wide
2½ yards of 1½" wide mauve sheer
   wire-edged ribbon
one 9"x5"x4" block of floral foam for
   drieds, serrated knife
24-gauge wire, floral tape
low temperature glue gun and sticks

Elegant Basket

1 Glue the foam into the bottom of the basket. Cut the ambrosinia
   into 8"–18" sprigs and glue evenly spaced into the foam, with the
taller sprigs in the center, extending upward, and the shorter ones
around the outside, extending outward and forward.

2 Cut the bay leaves into 6"–15" sprigs and glue into the foam as for
   the ambrosinia. Cut the achillia into 6"–18" sprigs and repeat.

3 Attach a wire stem to each hydrangea head with floral tape (see page 28) then cut nine into 8" sprigs and two into 14" sprigs. Glue the two 14" sprigs 6" apart into the foam center. Glue two 8" sprigs 6" apart into the foam at the basket back; repeat in the basket front. Insert a sprig at each end of the basket, and the last three along the front edge. Curve the second and fourth sprigs downward so the blossoms extend over the basket sides.

4 Cut the heather into 7"–18" sprigs and insert evenly spaced near materials of similar lengths and angled in the same direction. Angle the sprigs in the front and back of the arrangement outward.

5 Cut an 18" daisy sprig. Cut the remaining daisies into eight 7", seven 12" and six 14" sprigs. Glue the 18" sprig into the center, extending upward. Glue the 14" sprigs 4" away from the first sprig, all evenly spaced around the 18" sprig and extending upward. Glue the 12" then 7" sprigs around the 14" sprigs 4" away, evenly spaced and angled outward. Repeat with the 7" sprigs.

6 Cut the snapdragons into one 18", two 14" and three 11" sprigs. Glue the 18" sprig into the center, extending upward. Glue the two 14" sprigs into the foam 4" to the right and left of center, extending outward and forward. Insert one 11" sprig at the far right, one at the far left and one at the center front, all extending parallel with the table.

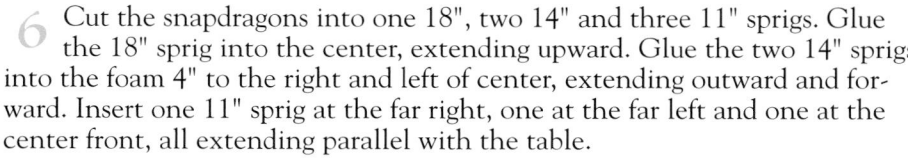

7 Lengthen the rose stems with wire as for the hydrangeas. Cut them into two 14" and three 12" sprigs. Insert a 14" sprig 3" to the right and left of the center snapdragon, angled away from it. Insert a 12" sprig in the center front of the arrangement, extending forward. Insert the other two 12" sprigs below and 6" to each side of the center rose, extending as for the nearby materials.

8 Cut the plumosus into 6"–20" sprigs and glue evenly spaced among materials of similar lengths, following the lines of the arrangement. Cut the lavender into 6"–15" sprigs and glue as for the plumosus.

9 Cut a 32" ribbon length. Wrap it around the basket with the ends at the center front and glue to secure. Use the remaining ribbon to make a puffy bow (see page 32) with a center loop, two 2½" loops, six 3½" loops and no tails. Glue the bow to the front center of the basket.

Rye Vase

one 3½"x8" glass cylinder vase
7 stems of red dried roses, each 1½" wide
6 oz. of dried rye
3 oz. of green preserved lecchio
2 oz. of yellow preserved genista
2 oz. of blue preserved misty limonium
2 oz. of purple preserved rice flower
1 oz. of dried raffia
2 medium-weight rubber bands
one 7½"x3" block of floral foam for drieds, serrated
   knife
low temperature glue gun and sticks

1 Trim the foam to fit into the vase and glue in place. Wrap the rubber bands around the vase, one 2" from the top and the other 2" from the bottom. Set aside 16–18 rye stems for step 2. Insert the remaining rye stems, one at a time, under the rubber bands, pushing the stems together to stand side by side. Continue all the way around until the vase is covered, then trim the stems even with the base of the vase.

2 Wrap three strands of raffia around the upper rubber band, cross the ends in front, wrap once more and tie in front. Trim the raffia ends to 1". Repeat over the lower rubber band. Cut the remaining rye into 8"–14" sprigs and insert into the foam with the longest stems at the center back, extending upward, and the shorter ones near the front, extending outward.

3 Cut one rose to 12", one to 11", one to 10", one to 9" and three to 7". Insert the 12" rose at the center and the 7" roses evenly spaced around the front. Glue the remaining three roses evenly spaced between the 12" and 7" roses, with the 9" rose at the left, the 11" rose at the right at the 10" rose in front. Cut the lecchio into 5"–9" sprigs and insert evenly spaced among the other materials with the longer sprigs in the center and back.

4 Cut the genista into 7"–12" sprigs and insert into the foam with the longest stems toward the center and back, extending upward, and the shorter ones around the front and sides, extending outward. Cut the limonium and the rice flower into 5"–10" sprigs and repeat, filling empty areas.

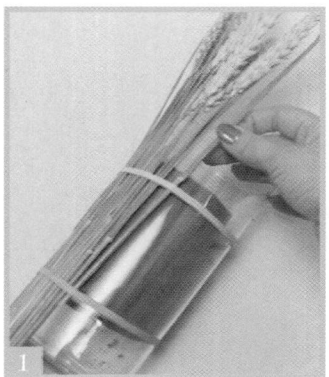

Garden Rocker

one 6½"x12"x12" white wicker rocking
   chair
one 5½" wide purple sinamay hat
2 oz. of green preserved lecchio
2 oz. of pink preserved leptospermum
2 oz. of purple preserved lavender
2 oz. of blue preserved misty limonium
2 oz. of white dried baby everlastings
½ yard of ¼" wide white satin ribbon
one 2"x2" cube of floral foam for drieds
low temperature glue gun and sticks

1   Glue the foam to the back left of
   the chair seat. Cut the lecchio into
3"–5" sprigs. Insert them into the foam
with the 5" sprigs at the back, extending upward, and the front, extending
across the seat. Insert the shorter sprigs
in the space between, extending as
shown.

2   Cut the leptospermum into 2"–5"
   sprigs; set aside four blossoms for
step 4. Glue the rest evenly spaced
among materials of similar lengths. Cut
the limonium into 2"–5" sprigs and
insert as for the leptospermum.

3   Cut the lavender into 3"–6" sprigs
   and the everlastings into 2" sprigs.
Glue all the sprigs evenly spaced among
materials of similar lengths.

4   Tie the ribbon around the hat at
   the base of the crown, knotting and gluing to secure. Glue the leptospermum blossoms from step 2 in a cluster
around the knot and glue the hat to the chair back as shown.

Devonshire Garden Basket

one 10"x4" brown willow basket with an 8" tall
   handle
16 stems of red dried roses, each 1½" wide
2 stems of yellow dried yarrow
2 oz. of green preserved plumosus fern
2 oz. of dark blue dried larkspur
2 oz. of dried caspia
2 oz. of white preserved sinuata statice
1 oz. of green sphagnum moss
two 2" long white/ivory mushroom birds
2 yards of ¼" wide white satin ribbon
24-gauge wire
low temperature glue gun and sticks

3   Cut the yarrow into 1" long sprigs and separate the
    blossoms into ⅓"–1" wide clusters. Glue three
evenly among the roses in each cluster. Break the moss
into 2" wide tufts and glue tufts to the basket rim
between the clusters. Glue a tuft to the basket handle
on each side of the fern.

4   Cut the statice into ½"–1" long sprigs and glue five
    sprigs evenly spaced among each floral cluster. Glue
a bird to the center handle top and one to the lower left
rim. Use the ribbon to make a loopy bow (see page 33)
with six 3" loops and two 14" tails. Glue it under the
rose on the basket handle and loop a tail around each
side of the handle. Glue the ends to secure.

1   Cut the plumosus fern into 3"–8" sprigs. Glue a
    cluster of 6–8 sprigs to the center handle top,
extending toward the sides. Glue the remaining sprigs
in six clusters of 6–8 sprigs evenly spaced around the
basket rim, extending as shown. Cut the roses to 2" and
glue in alternating clusters of two and three to the center of the fern clusters. Glue one rose to the cluster center on the handle top.

2   Cut the larkspur into 2" sprigs and glue three
    sprigs evenly around the roses in each cluster. Cut
the caspia into 4"–8" sprigs and glue around the roses in
each cluster, some extending outward and some upward.

Larkspur Birdhouse

one 8¼"x16"x6¼" wood birdhouse with fence and circular
   twig vine attached
9 stems of pink dried roses, each 1½" wide
one 4" wide blue preserved hydrangea blossom head
3 oz. of green preserved lecchio
2 oz. of green mood moss
2 oz. of purple dried larkspur
2 oz. of pink preserved misty limonium
1¼ yards of ⅝" wide burgundy taffeta wire-edged ribbon
three 2" long mauve mushroom birds
24-gauge wire
low temperature glue gun and sticks

1 Break the moss into 2"x4" tufts and save one for
   step 4. Glue the rest around the birdhouse to create the "yard." Insert a few tufts onto the lower area of
the vine that encircles the house. Cut the plumosus
into 4"–6" sprigs and glue evenly spaced around the
yard and onto vine from 12:00 to 6:00.

2 Cut the larkspur into one 13", one 11" and fourteen 5" sprigs. Glue the 13" sprig into the moss at
the right front house corner, extending upward through
the vine loop. Glue the 11" sprig to the right of it,
extending upward. Glue two 5" sprigs into each back
yard corner. Glue the remaining sprigs into the right
front corner around the longer sprigs, extending outward and forward as shown. Cut one rose to 9", one to
7", one to 5" and six to 4". Glue three 4" roses into the
moss at the left front corner. Glue the 9" rose in front of
the 13" larkspur with the 7" rose in front and left of it.
Glue the 5" rose to the left of the 7" rose and the
remaining 4" roses to the right of them.

3 Cut the limonium and the lecchio into 4"–8" sprigs
   and glue evenly spaced among materials of similar
lengths. Use the ribbon to make a loopy bow (see page
33) with four 2" loops, a 15" tail and an 11" tail. Glue it
to the birdhouse roof at the lower left. Extend the 15" tail
down to the house side and around to the fence front;
glue to secure. Extend the 11" tail upward, wrapping it
around the vine and securing at the top of the house.

4 Cut the hydrangea head into 2" sprigs and glue one
   to the fence top at the left front corner. Glue the
rest evenly spaced throughout the materials at the right
front corner. Glue the tuft of moss saved in step 1 to the
bottom of the birdhouse hole, then glue a mushroom bird
into the hole. Glue the others to the top left fence corner, spaced 1" apart as shown in the large photo.

Boxwood Topiary

one 7½"x3"x6" rectangular wood container
4 oz. of green preserved boxwood
ten 12" long dried birch twigs
3 oz. of purple preserved sinuata statice
3 oz. of dark mauve preserved heather
3 oz. of lavender preserved peppergrass
3 oz. of pink dried pepperberries
3 oz. of pink preserved leptospermum
1 oz. of green sphagnum moss
one 9"x5"x4" block of floral foam for drieds,
    serrated knife
low temperature glue gun and sticks

1   Cut 3" off one end of the foam block
    and glue it into the center of the container. Cover the foam with moss and tuck it into the space between the foam and the container. Insert the birch twigs evenly spaced into the foam center, extending upward. Round the edges of the remaining piece of foam and gently push it down over the tops of the birch twigs about 1" until firmly in place.

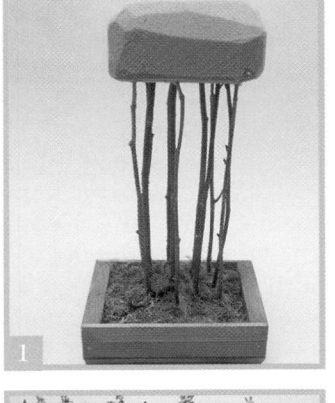

2   Cut ⅔ of the boxwood into 2½"–3" sprigs and the remaining ⅓ into 4" sprigs. Insert the 2½"–3" sprigs and half of the 4" sprigs evenly spaced over the entire upper block of foam. Insert the remaining 4" sprigs into the bottom foam among the twigs, extending upward.

3   Cut the statice into 3" sprigs and insert five around the base of the topiary. Insert the remaining sprigs evenly spaced into the top foam block. Cut the heather into 4"–5" sprigs and repeat.

4   Cut the pepperberries into 3" sprigs and insert evenly spaced among the materials in the upper foam, extending outward. Cut the peppergrass into 4" sprigs. Insert a few sprigs around the topiary base, extending upward. Insert the remaining sprigs evenly spaced into the upper foam as for the pepperberries. Cut the leptospermum into 5"–7" sprigs and glue as for the peppergrass.

Rose Flourish

one 5¾"x4"x2" green
  rectangular plastic
  floral container
5 stems of pink
  preserved roses, each
  2" wide
3 oz. of green preserved
  salal
3 oz. of green
  preserved bracken fern
3 oz. of purple
  preserved rice flower
3 oz. of pink preserved
  pepperberries
2 oz. of light green
  preserved lepidium
2 oz. of green
  preserved plumosus
  fern
2 oz. of white dried
  rhodanthe
2 oz. of pink preserved
  genista
one 5½"x4"x2" block of
  floral foam for drieds
low temperature glue
  gun and sticks

1   Glue the foam into the container. Cut the salal into 4"–6" sprigs and
    insert evenly spaced into the foam, extending outward, with the center
sprigs extending upward. Cut the bracken fern into 4"–6" sprigs and insert into
the foam, extending as for the salal to conceal the foam.

2   Cut the plumosus into 5"–8" sprigs and insert evenly spaced among the
    other materials. Cut the pepperberries into 5"–6" sprigs and glue evenly
spaced around the outer foam edge, extending over the side of the container.
Cut the roses to 5"–6" and glue evenly spaced among the other materials as
shown.

3   Cut the lepidium into 4"–8" sprigs and glue evenly spaced among the
    other materials, the sprigs around the outside edge extending outward and
the sprigs on top upward. Cut the rhodanthe into 5" sprigs and repeat.

4   Cut the rice flower into 4" sprigs and glue as for the lepidium. Cut the
    genista into 6"–8" sprigs and repeat, filling any empty areas.

A flair
with the Natural

Unpainted, undyed and unpretentious. While natural florals aren't glitzy or bright, they are the "binding" element in floral designing—they work with other elements to achieve an overall effect. The "naturals" category encompasses materials of natural shades, including grains and grasses, dried fruits and berries, mosses, mushrooms, lichens, twigs, branches and forest-grown materials. When combined in designs, the variety of textures and shadings commands attention.

Natural designs enhance and complement many different decorating styles because of their muted tones. In addition, arrangements made with naturals can be wonderful gifts for men.

When working with grains and grasses, it's important to use varying textures. The Baby's Breath Wreath (page 102) contains florals of similar colors, but the variety of textures adds depth and interest, while the rich brown ribbon, cones and cattails make striking complements to the natural tones. The cones and papaver pods in the Gathering Basket (page 107) bring the eye inward, becoming intriguing focal points. The Textured Arrangement (page 108) uses okra, jacaranda and lotus pods to bring order and balance to the wild grasses and grains of the background.

Naturals make great fillers for arrangements; their soft hues work with many color schemes, and they add mass and volume to a design. The vast array of available pods and cones can add texture and interest to a design—and because they look fresh when dried or preserved, they look great in many arrangements.

When choosing a container or base for a neutral or light-colored design, keep in mind that it should strengthen the overall feeling. Twiggy or leafy baskets, wood containers and birch or grapevine wreaths will enhance natural designs.

one 16" wide mini baby's breath wreath
4 oz. of dried black bearded wheat
4 oz. of dried poa grass
five 2"–2½" wide cedar roses on stems
4 oz. of brown dried cattails
2 oz. of dried bell reed
2 oz. of dried lagurus
2 oz. of dried brisa maxima
2⅛ yards of 1½" wide brown taffeta wired ribbon
18" of 22-gauge wire
low temperature glue gun and sticks

1 Cut the wheat into 6" sprigs. Glue five clusters of three evenly spaced around the inner wreath, angled counterclockwise. Glue 5-sprig clusters around the outer edge between the 3-sprig clusters, angled the same way. Cut the poa into 5" sprigs and glue ten clusters of 8–12 sprigs evenly spaced around the wreath, alternating them between the inner and outer edges.

2 Cut the cedar roses to 4" long and glue them evenly spaced around the wreath front. Cut the cattails to 6" long. Glue a cluster of three cattails behind each rose, extending outward and angled counterclockwise. Glue single cattails between the roses on the inside wreath edge, angled as for the other cattails.

3 Cut the bell reed into 4"–6" sprigs and glue in clusters of 6–10 sprigs throughout the design, angling them counterclockwise, extending alternately to the inside and outside. Cut the lagurus into 4" sprigs; glue clusters of 6–10 sprigs as for the bell reed.

4 Cut the brisa into 4"–6" sprigs and glue as for the bell reed. Use the ribbon to make a puffy bow (see page 32) with a center loop, four 3½" loops and one 42" tail. Glue the bow at 7:00, angled slightly left, and weave the tail among the florals around the wreath. Attach a wire hanger (see page 26) to the top back.

Natural Garland

3 oz. of raffia, 60" long
4 oz. of dried avena
2 oz. of lavender dried achillea
3 oz. of green dried silene grass

3 oz. of dried poa grass
5 oz. of purple dried oregano
3 yards of 1" wide olive green woven wired paper ribbon
22-gauge wire, wire cutters
low temperature glue gun and sticks

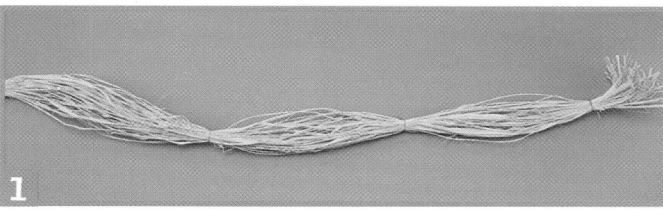

1 Hold the raffia at one end and shred it with your fingernail, separating the strands. Wire the strands together 3" from one end. Wire them together every 9" down the length of the raffia until you have six 9" sections and two 3" ends. Attach wire hangers (see page 26) behind the center wire and each end wire.

2 Cut the avena into 4"–6" sprigs. Glue 8–9 sprigs to the center wire, angled to the right; repeat, angling these left. Divide the rest of the sprigs into four equal clusters and glue one to each wire, angled toward the ends. Cut the ribbon into three equal lengths and use each to make a puffy bow (see page 32) with a center loop, four 2½" loops and 5" tails. Glue one to the center wire and one to each end wire.

3 Cut the silene, achillea and poa into 4"–5" sprigs. Glue a few sprigs of each among the bow loops. Glue the remaining silene evenly spaced among the avena sprigs, following the same angles. Divide the remaining achillea into four equal clusters and glue one on the inside of each avena cluster, covering the stems. Repeat with the remaining poa, but tuck the poa stems under the avena heads at the outside of each cluster.

4 Cut the oregano into 4"–5" sprigs. Glue in clusters to cover any visible raffia, angling each cluster toward the garland end.

Cornucopia

one 12"x7" vine cornucopia
three 2" wide dried pomegranates
six 1"–1½" wide mini lotus pods on stems
3 oz. of dried mini millet
2 oz. of dried wheat
2 oz. of purple dried oregano
2 oz. of green/orange dried safflowers
2 oz. of red dried hanging amaranthus

3 oz. of pink dried pepperberries
2 oz. of green mood moss
1 oz. of green sheet moss
one 4"x4"x4" block of floral foam for drieds
2½ yards of 1" wide tan/burgundy/green
   fabric ribbon
6" of 22-gauge wire
low temperature glue gun and sticks

1 Glue the foam into the cornucopia. Tuck sheet moss around the outside of the foam. Cut the wheat into 6"–8" sprigs and insert them into the bottom center of the foam, extending forward. Cut the millet into 6"–8" sprigs and insert half into the foam on each side of the wheat, angling slightly toward the sides.

2 Cut the oregano into 3"–9" sprigs and insert them into the foam, beginning between the wheat and the right millet with the longest sprigs, working upward and ending with the shortest sprigs at the top of the cornucopia. Glue the pomegranates in a triangle at the center top of the foam.

3 Cut the safflowers into 4"–7" sprigs and insert to the right of the oregano, again working from bottom to top and from long to short. Cut the pepperberries into 4"–6" sprigs. Glue a 5" sprig in the center of the cornucopia angled downward. Glue a 4" sprig over the pomegranates, extending downward. Glue the remaining pepperberries into the left side as for the safflowers.

4 Use the ribbon to make an oblong bow (see page 32) with a center loop, four 3" loops, six 5" loops and no tails. Glue it 4" below and left of the pomegranates. Cut the lotus pods to 6" long. Insert one below the bow and the rest clustered above the bow. Cut the amaranthus into 7" sprigs and insert them evenly spaced across the center bottom of the design to extend forward onto the table. Glue 1" tufts of mood moss throughout the design.

Birch Arch

one 28" wide birch twig arch
4 oz. of dried linum
4 oz. of green dried setaria
4 oz. of light green dried avena
4 oz. of dried black bearded
  wheat
3 oz. of purple dried oregano
3 oz. of green dried silene grass
3 oz. of dried papaver
3 oz. of dried lagurus
2 oz. of green preserved hops
2 oz. of dried barley
4 oz. of green preserved salal
3 oz. of green preserved
  dudinea
five 1"–2" wide dried mini
  lotus pods
22-gauge wire, wire cutters
low temperature glue gun and
  sticks

1 Cut the linum into 10" sprigs. Divide it in half and wire each half together 1" from the cut ends to make two clusters. Repeat with the avena and setaria. Glue a linum cluster to each end of the arch, extending over the twig ends at the same angle. Glue a setaria and an avena cluster 5" above each linum cluster, angling the setaria to the outside and the avena to the inside of the arch.

2 Cut the wheat into 10" sprigs and divide it in half, wiring each half to make a cluster. Cut the oregano and silene into 8" sprigs, divide and wire as for the wheat. Glue a wheat cluster above the setaria on each side, angled outward. Glue an oregano cluster below each wheat cluster and to the inside of the arch. Glue a silene cluster above and to the outside of each oregano cluster.

3 Cut the papaver into 4"–7" sprigs, divide and wire as for the previous materials. Glue one on each arch side to extend between the silene and oregano. Cut the lagurus into 4"–7" sprigs, divide and wire, then glue a cluster to extend from the arch center toward each end. Glue the hops in the arch center as shown.

4 Cut the barley into 4"–5" sprigs, divide, wire and glue one cluster above each lagurus cluster. Cut the salal and dudinea into 6" sprigs and insert them throughout the design to fill empty areas, following the angles of the nearby materials. Glue the lotus pods among the hops as shown. Attach a wire hanger (see page 26) to the top back.

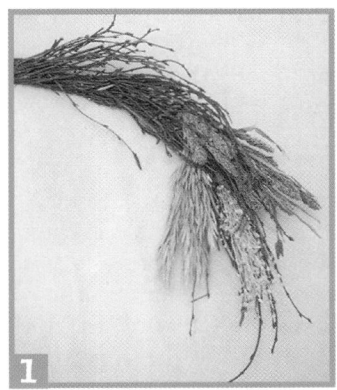

Fall Forest Bouquet

one 24"x18" twig wall pocket
4 oz. of dried setaria
4 oz. of green preserved oak leaves
4 oz. of dried wheat
2 oz. of dried festuca grass
4 oz. of red preserved myrtle
2 oz. of green lecchio
6 oz. of red dried pepperberries
3 oz. of white dried button flowers
3 oz. of dried rice grass
three 3"–4" wide sponge mushrooms
3"x3"x2" block of floral foam for drieds
1 oz. of green sheet moss
22-gauge wire, wire cutters
low temperature glue gun and sticks

1 Attach a wire hanger (see page 26) to the center back of the twig pocket. Insert the foam, trimming the bottom as needed to fit. Push moss behind the twigs in front to conceal the foam. Cut the setaria into 5"–15" sprigs and insert them into the foam on the center right side as shown, with the longest sprigs at the back and the shortest in front. Insert a few sprigs between the twigs of the pocket. Repeat with the oak leaves, inserting them in the center of the foam with some shorter sprigs among and right of the setaria sprigs.

2 Cut the wheat into 5"–13" sprigs and insert them into the foam on the left side of the pocket with shorter sprigs in front. Cut the festuca into 5"–14" sprigs and insert them evenly spaced throughout the arrangement with shorter sprigs in front. Cut the myrtle into 5"–9" sprigs and insert them throughout the front and center of the arrangement as shown.

3 Glue the mushrooms to the outside lower left of the pocket as shown. Cut the pepperberries into 5"–12" sprigs and glue one sprig among the mushrooms, angled downward. Glue the remaining pepperberries evenly spaced around the outer edges of the design.

4 Cut the button flowers into 6"–10" sprigs, divide and wire them into eight equal clusters. Glue them throughout the lower half of the arrangement as shown. Cut the lecchio into 4"–6" sprigs and glue half on the lower right side of the mushrooms, angled outward. Glue ¼ at the lower left of and the rest at the upper left of the mushrooms. Cut the rice grass into 5"–15" sprigs and insert evenly spaced throughout the arrangement.

Gathering Basket

one 15"x8" gathering basket with a 4" tall handle
two 3½" long pine cones, three 2"–3" wide dried whole oranges
2 oz. of dried avena
4 oz. of dried mini millet
3 oz. of dried barley
2 oz. of dried silene grass
3 oz. of dried blonde wheat
1 oz. of dried rice grass
2 oz. of dried papaver
4 oz. of red dried pepperberries
2 oz. of green mood moss
one 6"x4"x2" block of floral foam for drieds
22-gauge wire, wire cutters, low temperature glue gun and sticks

1 Glue the foam into the basket center. Divide the avena in half and wire each bunch ⅓ of the way down the stems. Glue the wired areas to the foam with one bunch extending each way, angled slightly forward. Trim any stems that hang over the basket edge. Repeat with the millet, gluing the bunches behind the avena.

2 Cut the barley stems to 3"–4". Insert into the back of the design in a fan. Wire the silene grass under the heads and cut the stems off below the wire. Glue them to the basket center over the right avena bunch, angled downward in front of the avena.

3 Wire the wheat together under the heads; cut the stems below the wire. Glue the wheat over the silene angled left. Wire and trim the rice grass as for the wheat; glue it behind the wheat at a similar angle. Glue a cone on each side as shown.

4 Glue two oranges, one above the other, to the front of the arrangement just right of the handle. Glue the remaining orange left of the left pine cone. Cut the papaver into 3"–6" sprigs and glue in clusters of three, one to the left of the left orange, one in front of the left pine cone and one to the right of the right oranges. Glue the pepperberries and moss evenly spaced among the papaver, oranges and pine cones.

Textured Arrangement

one 8"x6"x4" oval vine basket with
  woven twigs
4 oz. of blond dried christina grass
3 oz. of light green dried setaria
4 oz. of brown dried cattails
8 oz. of white dried margaritas
4 oz. of green dried avena
2 oz. of green preserved hops
five 3"–5" long okra pods on stems
three 3" wide lotus pods on picks
seven 2½"–3" long jacaranda pods on
  stems
three 2" wide rope balls on stems
3 oz. of green sheet moss
4"x4"x5" block of floral foam for drieds
low temperature glue gun and sticks

1 Glue the foam into the basket. Cut the setaria into 10"–17" sprigs. Insert a cluster of four 16"–17" sprigs at the center back of the foam. Insert a cluster of four 13"–15" sprigs 3" away on each side of the first, angled slightly outward. Insert four clusters of 10"–12" sprigs evenly spaced across the front of the foam. Cut the christina grass into 8"–16" sprigs and insert them among the setaria near stems of similar lengths.

2 Cut one okra pod to 14", two to 16" and two to 10" long. Insert the 14" pod at the center of the foam, angled upward. Insert a 10" sprig at each front corner of the foam and a 16" sprig at each back corner, all angled outward. Cut the cattails into 10"–20" sprigs and insert them evenly spaced among the previous materials at similar heights and angles.

3 Insert the lotus pods in a cluster at the left front. Cut the rope ball stems to 10" and insert them in a cluster above and behind the lotus pods. Cut four jacaranda pods to 6" long, two to 8" and one to 12". Insert them clustered at the right front of the arrangement, with taller ones behind shorter stems.

4 Divide the margaritas into 3" wide clusters, cut the clusters to 6"–15" long and insert them evenly spaced throughout the arrangement. Cut the avena into 6"–16" sprigs and insert them to fill empty areas. Insert moss among the lower stems to conceal the foam. Glue the hops in a cluster to the basket front.

Forest Wreath

one 18" birch twig wreath
three 2"–3" wide brown dried lotus pods
3 oz. of green preserved bracken fern
3 oz. of red preserved bracken fern
3 oz. of preserved avena
3 oz. of blue preserved heather
3 oz. of preserved baby's breath
3 oz. of dried brisa maxima
3 oz. of green oak leaves
4 stems of red latex raspberries, each
    with 2 clusters of five ⅝" long berries
    and many 1" wide leaves
6" of 22-gauge wire
low temperature glue gun and sticks

1 Attach a wire hanger (see page 26) to the top back of the wreath. Cut the green fern into 6" sprigs and glue them clockwise around the wreath, angling them alternately inward and outward. Glue a lotus pod at 11:00 angled outward, one at 3:00 angled downward and one at 8:00 angled upward.

2 Cut the avena into 5"–7" sprigs and glue them evenly spaced around the wreath, angled clockwise. Cut the heather into 4"–8" sprigs and glue as for the avena.

3 Cut the baby's breath into 3"–5" sprigs and glue them evenly spaced among the fern sprigs, extending clockwise. Cut the berries into eight 4" long 5-berry sprigs and glue them evenly spaced around the wreath, angled clockwise.

4 Cut the red fern into 4"–6" sprigs and glue them evenly spaced among the previous materials, extending clockwise. Cut the brisa maxima and oak leaves into 3"–6" sprigs and glue them as for the red fern sprigs.

Pressed and Pretty

Crafting with pressed flowers is a pastime often associated with the Victorian era or with particular memories. The first rose from a true love or from a wedding bouquet, a flower picked from a special wreath are mementos which provide reasons to press flowers. The projects included on the following pages feature pressed flowers added as decorative floral accents to objects found in craft stores.

Flat surfaces which will have limited use can be embellished with pressed flowers. They can be applied to glass for a lovely wall hanging, glued to the corners or around the frame of plain mirrors to add a romantic touch. A few blossoms cascading down the front of a white glass vase can give the illusion of hand painting. The addition of pressed flowers can turn a simple, functional article into a charming decorative element. When the Birdhouse Lamp (page 118) is lit, the leaves cast intriguing shapes and diffuse the soft glow of the light, adding to the beauty of the piece. The Meadow Clock (page 112) is another example of an item that is as beautiful as it is functional when decorated with pressed flowers.

Decorating stationery and paper goods is one of the simplest ways to use pressed flowers. Glue your favorite pressed flower to plain white paper to create personalized stationery. Use a few leaves and blossoms to decorate announcements and cards, make gift bags or embellish bookmarks. Turn a photograph into a special gift by putting it in the charming Picture Frame (page 116). Gifts decorated and embellished with pressed flowers will become cherished keepsakes.

Meadow Clock

one 6½"x10" wood-framed clock
pressed materials:
- three 4" long magenta bellflower sprigs
- two 4½" long stems of lavender shooting stars
- two 2" long stems of lavender salvia blossoms
- two ⅝" wide yellow viola blossoms
- eight ⅝" wide purple alyssum blossoms
- eighteen 1" long tamarac sprigs
- twelve 1½"–3" long green poppy leaves
- sixteen ½"–1½" long green larkspur leaves

ivory acrylic paint
wood spray sealer
matte finish acrylic spray sealer
paintbrushes: #4 flat, 1" wide sponge
fine sandpaper
thin craft glue
tweezers (for moving and placing blossoms)
soft cloth

1 Remove the clockworks. Sand the clock lightly and clean with the soft cloth. Apply a coat of wood sealer; let dry. Use the sponge brush to paint it with two coats of ivory; let dry. Use the flat paintbrush to apply glue to the backs of the poppy leaves and glue them to the clock front as shown.

2 Glue half of the larkspur leaves to the clock, extending upward. Glue the rest to the base, extending forward. Glue a magenta bellflower among the lower poppy leaves on each side of the clock front. Cut the blossoms off the remaining sprig and glue the individual blossoms among the clock front poppy leaves as shown.

3 Glue the shooting stars to the center front, extending upward away from each other, with their stems together at the base. Glue a salvia blossom on each side of the shooting stars as shown.

4 Glue a yellow viola to the right and left of the salvia, touching the clock base. Glue the alyssum across the bottom and base. Glue the tamarac evenly spaced among the alyssum and violas. Spray the piece with the acrylic sealer, then replace the clockworks.

Garden Footstool

one 12"x8"x9" pine footstool
pressed materials:

- two 1"–1¼" wide purple/yellow pansy blossoms
- four ¾"–1" wide purple viola blossoms
- two ¾"–1" wide yellow/purple viola blossoms
- two ¾"–1" wide yellow viola blossoms
- four 2" long lavender/white salvia blossoms
- six ½"–1" long lavender/white salvia blossoms
- fourteen ½"–¾" wide dark pink alyssum blossoms
- six ¼"–½" wide yellow golden aster blossoms
- twelve ½" wide purple verbena blossoms
- eight sprigs of green maidenhair fern: two 5" long, two 4" long, four 3" long

paintbrushes: #4 flat, 1" wide sponge
tweezers (for moving and placing blossoms)
ivory acrylic paint
wood spray sealer
matte finish acrylic spray sealer
fine sandpaper
thin craft glue
soft cloth

1   Sand the stool lightly and clean with the soft cloth. Apply a coat of wood sealer; let dry. Use the sponge brush to paint the stool with two coats of ivory paint; let dry. Use the flat paintbrush to apply glue to the backs of the two 4" fern sprigs. Place on the stool top at the lower center, extending in opposite directions. Glue two 5" fern sprigs to the upper center stool top, extending as before. Glue a 3" fern sprig above and one below each 5" sprig, extending as shown.

2   Glue a pansy to the center of each fern spray. Glue a purple viola 2" to each side of the lower pansy and ¾" to each side of the upper pansy. Glue a yellow viola above and below each of the upper violas as shown. Glue a purple/yellow viola 1½" from each end of the upper fern spray.

3   Glue a 2" salvia blossom on each side of the bottom pansy, one extending toward each end. Glue four ½"–1" salvia sprigs around the upper pansy. Glue a 1" sprig between the purple and purple/yellow violas. Glue a 2" salvia sprig below each purple/yellow viola, angled downward. Glue the alyssum sprigs evenly spaced among the other materials at similar angles.

4   Glue four aster blossoms evenly spaced around the lower middle viola. Glue one aster in the middle of each lower fern sprig. Glue the verbena evenly spaced among all the other materials, with four in the lower group and eight in the upper group; seal. (Use polymer sealer if the footstool is to be used for other than decorative purposes.)

Framed Wreath

one 10½"x12½" gold/black oval photo frame
   with a glass front
one 8"x10" piece of ivory cotton fabric
pressed materials:
- thirteen 1" wide purple viola blossoms
- two 1" wide white larkspur blossoms
- four 1" wide blue larkspur blossoms
- three 1" wide pink larkspur blossoms
- eleven ½" wide red verbena blossoms
- thirteen ¼" wide blue verbena blossoms
- seven 1½" wide pink shooting star blossoms
- twelve 1" wide white bridal wreath blossoms
- two 3" long sprigs of green rabbit's foot fern

1 yard of ¼" wide lavendar satin ribbon
pencil
thin craft glue
#4 flat paintbrush
tweezers (for moving and placing blossoms)

1 Remove the frame insert and glue the fabric to the side that faces forward. Cut the excess fabric from the edges of the insert. Lightly trace an oval onto the center of the fabric to serve as a guideline for gluing. Use the paintbrush to apply glue to the backs of the violas. Place a cluster of three violas at 11:00, one at 3:00 and one at 8:00. Glue the rest in pairs at 1:00 and 6:00.

2 Glue a larkspur blossom of each color in a cluster at 10:00 and at 2:00. Glue a blue larkspur at 12:00. Glue the remaining larkspur blossoms at 5:00. Glue the red verbenas to fill the spaces among the other materials, as shown.

3 Glue the blue verbena evenly spaced among the other materials. Cut the fronds off the fern and into 1" sprigs; glue evenly among the other materials.

4 Glue the shooting star blossoms evenly spaced among the other materials. Glue the bridal wreath blossoms among the other materials, alternating from the inside to outside edge. Cut a 2" ribbon length. Use the remaining ribbon to make a loopy bow (see page 33) with six 2" loops and two 5" tails, securing the bow with the 2" length. Glue to the top of the oval. Let the glue dry, then place inside the frame. (The large photo was shot without the protective glass to avoid glare.)

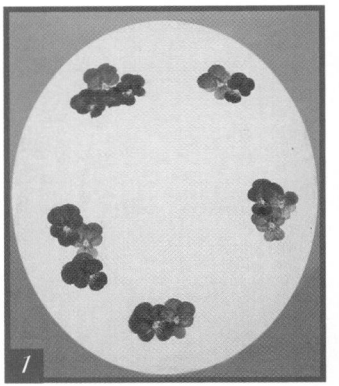

Satin Box

one 5½"x3"x3" oval white satin box
pressed materials:
- one 2" wide purple/white pansy blossom
- two 2" wide blue salvia blossoms
- two 1" wide blue salvia blossoms
- two 1" wide violet four o'clock blossoms
- three 1" wide violet alyssum blossoms
- five ½" wide white Queen Anne's lace blossoms
- twelve ½" long purple verbena blossoms
- six ½" long pink verbena blossoms
- seventeen ½"–1" long green ivy leaves
- six 1"–2" long sprigs of green rabbit's foot fern

½ yard of ⅝" wide mauve wire-edged taffeta ribbon
matte finish acrylic spray sealer
#4 flat paintbrush
thin craft glue
tweezers (for moving and placing blossoms)

1 Lay the pressed materials face up on a flat, covered surface and spray with several light coats of sealer; be sure to hold the sealer 12"–18" away to avoid blowing the blossoms off the surface. Use the paintbrush to apply glue to the back of the pansy and place in the center of the lid. Glue two 2" long fern sprigs on each side of the pansy, angled as shown. Glue the 1" fern sprig above the pansy, angling one right and one left. Glue six ivy leaves around the pansy as shown.

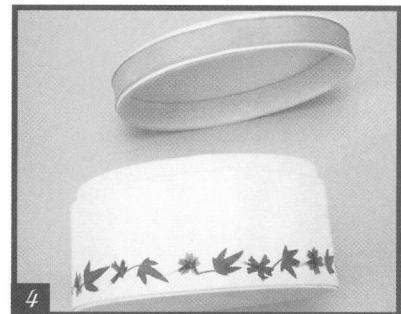

2 Glue a 2" salvia blossom on each side of the pansy, extending toward the end of the lid. Glue the 1" salvia blossoms below the 2" blossoms, angled downward. Glue a four o'clock blossom between the salvia blossoms on each side.

3 Glue the three alyssum blossoms evenly spaced just above the pansy. Glue the Queen Anne's lace evenly spaced around the pansy. Glue seven blue verbena blossoms evenly spaced on each side of and below the pansy.

4 Glue the ribbon around the side of the lid. Glue the remaining ivy leaves, blue and pink verbena evenly spaced around the bottom of the box, with an ivy leaf between the blossoms and alternating blossom colors.

one 8"x6½" unfinished wood picture frame with a 4½"x3" opening
pressed materials
- four ¾"–1" wide purple/yellow viola blossoms
- three 1" wide pink larkspur blossoms
- three 3" long white misty limonium sprigs
- ten ½"–¾" wide violet verbena blossoms
- fourteen ½" wide purple lobelia blossoms
- five 4" sprigs of green maidenhair fern
- four 1" sprigs of green maidenhair fern

wood spray sealer
matte finish acrylic spray sealer
#4 flat paintbrush
thin craft glue
tweezers (for moving and placing blossoms)

Picture Frame

1 Apply a coat of wood sealer; let dry. Use the paintbrush to apply glue to the back of a 4" fern sprig and place at the lower left of the frame, extending right. Glue two 4" sprigs at each upper corner of the frame, with one extending toward the opposite side and the other extending downward. Glue the four 1" sprigs extending from the bottom center to the bottom right, angling as shown.

2 Glue one viola to each upper fern cluster and one to the lower left fern cluster as shown. Glue the remaining viola over a lower 1" fern sprig as shown. Glue one larkspur blossom above the upper right viola; glue another blossom on each side of the viola at the lower left.

3 Cut the limonium into ½"–2" sprigs. Glue evenly spaced among the fern sprigs, extending in the same directions. Glue three verbena blossoms among each upper cluster as shown. Glue two verbenas near the larkspur at the lower left and the remaining two blossoms among the 1" fern sprigs.

4 Glue four lobelia blossoms evenly spaced among the upper right and the bottom cluster. Glue the remaining six blossoms evenly spaced to the upper left cluster. Let the glue dry completely then spray several thin coats of sealer over the surface of the frame, allowing the sealer to dry between coats.

Stationery

one 7"x5" blank card with a slightly larger envelope

pressed materials:
- four 1"–2" sprigs of green maidenhair fern
- four 1" wide yellow viola blossoms
- two 1" wide white/yellow daisy blossoms
- nine ¾" wide Queen Anne's lace blossoms
- two 2" long blue bluebell sprigs
- six 1" long blue bluebell blossoms
- four 2" long yellow sweet clover blossoms
- four 1" wide lavender honeysuckle blossoms

#4 flat paintbrush, thin craft glue
matte finish acrylic spray sealer
tweezers (for moving and placing blossoms)

1 Lay the pressed materials face up on a flat, covered surface and spray with several light coats of sealer; be sure to hold the sealer 12"–18" away to avoid blowing the blossoms off the surface. Use the paintbrush to apply glue to the backs of two 2" sprigs of fern. Place them on the card, curving upward and toward each other at the top. Set aside two 1" sprigs for step 2. Fill in the bottom space between the sprigs with the remaining sprigs, angled as shown. Glue a viola to the center bottom and to each side of the fern spray. Glue a daisy on each side of the center viola. Glue the Queen Anne's lace evenly spaced among the other materials.

2 Glue a 2" bluebell sprig and two bluebell blossoms to each upper side, extending upward as shown in the large photo. Glue two sweet clover blossoms near each daisy, angled toward the card side. Glue the honeysuckle along the bottom of the design as shown. Make a matching envelope seal with a viola, a bluebell blossom, and two 1" fern sprigs glued as shown.

one sheet of Paper Pizazz™ purple sponged print paper
one 2½"x 4½" piece of white paper
one 2½"x 4½" sheet of translucent vellum
"Friends" poem rub–on letters, from True Expressions™

pressed materials:
- two 1" wide purple/yellow viola blossoms
- four 1"–1½" long sprigs of larkspur leaves
- four ½" wide purple verbena blossoms

#4 flat paintbrush, thin craft glue
matte finish acrylic spray sealer
tweezers (for moving and placing blossoms)

1 Lay the pressed materials face up on a flat, covered surface and spray with several light coats of sealer; be sure to hold the sealer 12"–18" away to avoid blowing the blossoms off the surface. Cut the patterned paper to 6"x8½". Fold in half to make a 4¼"x6" card. Use the paintbrush to apply glue to the back of the viola blossoms. Place one at the top left and one at the lower right of the white paper. Following the directions given on the package, rub the printed phrase onto the center of the white paper.

2 Glue two larkspur leaf sprigs by the upper left blossom, one extending down and one to the right. Glue the other two by the lower right blossom, one extending up and one to the left. Glue a verbena blossom to the center of each leaf sprig. Run a thin bead of glue around the edge of the vellum and glue it over the top of the white paper. Glue the white paper centered onto the card.

Birdhouse Lamp

one 5"x17" wood birdhouse lamp with 7" wide shade
one 24"x12" sheet of handmade paper, beige with grassy
    fibers
one 24"x12" piece of white butcher paper
pressed materials:
  • fourteen 1¼"–2½" long maple leaves in fall tones
  • twelve 2"–3" long sprigs of green basil
  • six 2" long sprigs of red Indian paintbrush
  • six ¼"–½" wide sprigs of white Queen Anne's lace
  • six ½"–1" wide sprigs of white bridal wreath
acrylic paint:
  • ivory
  • tan
wood spray sealer
matte finish acrylic spray sealer
fine grit sandpaper
soft cloth
paintbrushes: #4 flat, 1" wide sponge
thin craft glue
tweezers (for moving and placing blossoms)
pencil

1 Lightly sand the birdhouse and clean with the soft cloth. Seal and let dry. Use the sponge brush to paint the walls, perches and underside of the roof with two coats of ivory. Paint the roof with two coats of tan; let dry.

2 Lay the lampshade on the butcher paper. Fit the paper to the shade; draw and cut a pattern, adding at least ¾" to the upper and lower edges and each end. Lay the pattern on the handmade paper, trace and cut it out. Glue one edge of the paper to the vertical seam on the lampshade. Wrap the paper around the lampshade, gluing and smoothing it as you go. Overlap the paper edges and glue the second one over the first.

3 Apply glue to the excess paper at the top and bottom of the shade, then fold to the underside of the lampshade; let dry. Use the flat paintbrush to apply glue to the backs of the fall leaves and place evenly spaced around the lampshade.

4 Cut the basil into ½"–1¼" sprigs and glue around the base of the birdhouse. Glue the bridal wreath, Indian paintbrush and Queen Anne's lace evenly spaced among the basil, alternating the sprig types; let dry. Lightly spray a coat of sealer over the birdhouse and lampshade.

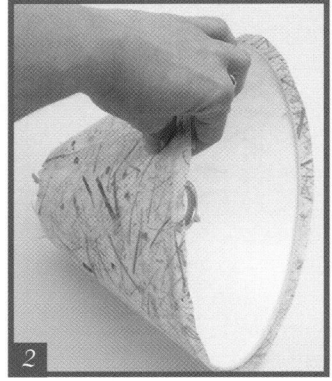
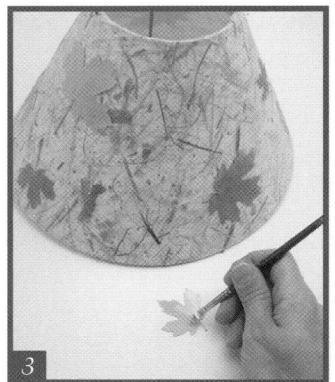

Memory Album

one 7"x10" spiral bound scrapbook with brown corrugated paper cover

pressed materials:
- seven 1"– 3" sprigs of green rabbit's foot fern
- five 1" wide yellow/purple viola blossoms
- five 1" wide purple alyssum blossoms
- five 2½" long yellow sweet clover blossoms
- fifteen ½"–¾" wide green ivy leaves
- eleven 1"–2" long blue bluebell sprigs
- seven 1" long dark pink boronia sprigs
- eight ½" wide dark pink verbena blossoms
- seven 1" wide white alyssum blossoms

one ¼" flat paintbrush
matte finish acrylic spray sealer
thin craft glue
tweezers (for moving and placing blossoms)

1 Lay the pressed materials face up on a flat, covered surface and spray with several light coats of sealer; be sure to hold the sealer 12"–18" away to avoid blowing the blossoms off the surface. Use the paintbrush to apply glue to the backs of the fern. Glue to the album cover in a heart shape. Glue the violas as shown.

2 Glue an alyssum blossom between the violas, angled outward. Cut each 2½" sweet clover blossom into one ½" and two 1" blossoms sprigs. Glue even-ly spaced around the heart, each angled diagonally across the materials as shown.

3 Glue the ivy leaves evenly spaced around the heart edges, alternating their angle as shown. Glue the bluebells to the heart as for the ivy.

4 Glue the boronia evenly spaced around the heart edges, alternating the angles. Glue the verbena and the white alyssum as for the boronia.

Floral Accents & Embellishments

Often a floral accent piece can add a special touch to a room. Using dried flowers to embellish boxes, frames and other decorative pieces can add polish to a home.

Old books are dressed up with florals and ribbon to become a pretty addition to a corner shelf, adding romance and a touch of color. A plain teacup and saucer become a charming accent by filling it with dried flowers. To bring a bit of the outdoors into a room, a frame for a mirror, a picture frame and a box have been decorated with a variety of mosses, along with twigs and pods. A great addition for the den or office!

It's easy to turn plain items into designer accents by embellishing them with dried materials. To carry the theme throughout the room, use the same floral materials and ribbon as touches or additions. The floral embellishment on the Heart-Shaped Box (page 127) could make a lovely curtain tieback by using the ribbon to tie the flowers together in a shoestring bow, keeping the tails long enough to pull back the curtain. In addition, the same amount of flowers, left on long stems, could be clustered into a hand-tied bouquet to be placed on a side table. Coordinating pieces by adding similar decorative touches helps unify the decor of a room.

The decorative touches found in this section could be adapted and constructed on other bases, giving each a whole new look and feeling. Experimenting with unusual items as bases can provide the perfect decorating piece for each room.

Decorated Shelf

one 23"x13½"x6" two-tier pine plate
  rack with towel bar
16 stems of red dried roses, each ¾"–1"
  wide
4 oz. of green preserved spiral eucalyptus
4 oz. of pink preserved heather
3 oz. of dried lilac achillia

3 oz. of purple preserved leptospermum
3 oz. of preserved baby's breath
2 oz. of mauve dried starflowers
one 8"x3"x5" block of floral foam for
  drieds
wood spray sealer
low temperature glue gun and sticks

1 Seal the plate rack; let dry. Glue the foam to the center of the lower
shelf. Cut the eucalyptus into 5"–8" sprigs. Glue the longer sprigs into
the ends of the foam and the shorter sprigs into the front and top. Cut the
achillia into 4"–8" sprigs and glue evenly spaced among the eucalyptus, near
sprigs of similar lengths and extending in the same direction.

2 Cut the roses to 4"–7" ;and glue evenly spaced into the foam, extending as
for the eucalyptus. Cut the starflowers into 4"–9" sprigs and glue evenly
spaced in clusters of 10–15 among other
materials of similar lengths.

3 Cut the leptospermum into 4"–7" sprigs
and the heather into 4"–9" sprigs.
Glue among the other materials.

4 Cut the baby's breath into 4"–7" sprigs
and glue evenly spaced among the other
materials, filling empty areas in the
arrangement.

Stacked Books

two 5½"x8½"x1" tan books
three 9" long dried pencil
    cattails
one 2" wide yellow dried
    yarrow blossom
2 oz. of green preserved oak
    leaves
2 oz. of yellow preserved
    leptospermum
1 oz. of dried festuca grass
1 oz. of dried achillia
1¾ yards of 1½" wide brown
    taffeta wire-edged ribbon
24-gauge wire
low temperature glue gun
    and sticks

For clarity, the instructions and step by step photos feature the books shown from the top, although when displayed they are viewed from the side.

1 Stack the books on top of each other. Cut a 16" length of ribbon and wrap it horizontally around the center of the books, gluing the ends together on top. Cut a 21" length of ribbon and wrap it vertically around the center of the books, gluing together over the ends of the first length. Use the remaining ribbon to make a collar bow (see page 34) with two 2¾" loops and two 5" tails. Glue it to the top of the books where the ribbons cross, with the tails extending downward.

2 Cut the oak leaves into 1½"–3" sprigs. Glue the 3" sprigs around the bow, extending from under the loops. Glue 1½" sprigs in the center of the bow, extending upward. Cut the festuca grass into 2"–4" sprigs and glue evenly spaced among both layers of oak leaves, extending in the same direction.

3 Glue the cattails over the bow, extending among the oak leaves as shown. Cut the achillia into 2"–4" sprigs and glue evenly spaced among the other materials.

4 Glue the yarrow blossom over the cattail stems where they cross. Cut the leptospermum into 2"–5" sprigs and glue evenly spaced among the other materials, extending in similar directions.

Victorian Potpourri

one 5"x5½" glass bowl-style vase
one 7" wide round ivory crocheted doily
one ¾" wide pink dried rose blossom
3 oz. of green/pink potpourri
1 oz. of pink preserved misty limonium
1 oz. of green preserved boxwood
1 yard of ⅝" wide mauve taffeta wire-edged ribbon
low temperature glue gun and sticks

1 Fill the vase with the potpourri. Center the doily over the opening, then secure the doily by tying the ribbon around the indentation just below the rim. Tie the ribbon tails into a shoestring bow (see page 35) with two 2" loops and 3½" tails.

2 Cut the boxwood into 2"–3" sprigs and glue evenly spaced among the bow loops, extending outward. Cut the limonium into 2"–3" sprigs and glue among the boxwood sprigs. Cut the stem off the rose and glue it to the center of the bow, extending forward.

Spicy Potpourri

one 3½"x7½"x3½" glass cylinder vase
5½" of 5" wide jute/wire mesh ribbon
1 yard of 1½" wide brown taffeta ribbon

3 stems of dried papaver
6 oz. of orange/brown potpourri
2 oz. of brown preserved lecchio
1 oz. of dried barley
1 oz. of mauve dried pepperberries
low temperature glue gun and sticks

1 Fill the vase with the potpourri. Stretch the mesh ribbon over the top and bend the excess to extend down over the sides. Trim the ribbon so that 1½" drapes over the sides all the way around. Wrap the taffeta ribbon around the vase 1" from the top and tie a shoestring bow (see page 35) to secure the mesh ribbon. Make the bow with two 2" loops and 6" tails.

2 Cut the papaver heads from the stems and glue to the bow center. Cut the barley into 2"–3" sprigs and glue around the papaver. Cut the lecchio into 3" sprigs and the pepperberries into 2"–3" sprigs and glue among the papaver as shown.

Cup & Saucer

one white/silver china cup and
  saucer set
6 stems of red dried roses, each ¾"
  wide
2 oz. of blue dried caspia
2 stems of green preserved leatherleaf fern
2 oz. of dried lavender
2 oz. of white dried ixodia daisy
2 oz. of pink dried larkspur
2 oz. of yellow preserved peppergrass
1 oz. of green sphagnum moss
one 3" cube of floral foam for
  drieds
low temperature glue gun and
  sticks

1 Glue the foam into the cup, then cover the foam with moss. Cut one rose to 4" and four to 3"; set aside the remaining rose for step 4. Insert the 4" rose into the center of the foam, extending upward. Insert the remaining roses evenly spaced around the outside edge of the foam, angling outward.

2 Cut the caspia into 3"–5" sprigs. Insert a row of shorter sprigs evenly spaced around the cup rim, extending outward. Insert the longer sprigs evenly spaced into the foam top, creating a dome shape. Set aside three remainder sprigs for step 4. Cut the fern into 3"–5" sprigs and glue as for the caspia; set aside three remainder sprigs for step 4.

3 Cut the lavender and daisies into 3"–5" sprigs and insert evenly near materials of similar lengths.

4 Cut the larkspur and peppergrass into 2"–5" sprigs and insert evenly spaced near materials of similar lengths. Glue any remaining 2" larkspur sprigs to the saucer as shown in the large photo. Cut the stem off the remaining rose. Glue it to the center of the saucer larkspur blossoms, then glue the saved sprigs of the other materials around the rose. (If desired, glue the cup to the saucer to secure.)

Tussie-Mussie

one 3"x7" white plaster tussie-mussie
   holder
8 stems of pink dried roses, each ¾"
   wide
one 4" wide purple dried hydrangea
   blossom head
2 oz. of green preserved plumosus fern
2 oz. of green preserved tree fern
1 oz. of preserved baby's breath
1 oz. of light blue dried larkspur
1 oz. of green sphagnum moss
1 yard of ¼" wide blue satin ribbon
one 3" cube of floral foam for drieds
serrated knife
24-gauge wire
low temperature glue gun and sticks

1 Cut the foam into a cone shape and glue inside the
tussie-mussie holder with three or four drops of
glue at the bottom. Tuck the moss between the holder
and the foam.

2 Cut the plumosus into 4"–6" sprigs and glue the
longer sprigs evenly spaced around the edge of the
holder, extending outward. Glue the remaining sprigs
evenly spaced in the center, concealing the foam and
extending forward. Repeat for the tree fern.

3 Cut one rose to 5" and seven to 3" or 4". Insert the
5" rose in the center of the foam, extending forward. Insert the remaining roses evenly spaced around
the edges of the foam, alternating lengths. Cut the
baby's breath into 2"–4" sprigs and glue evenly spaced
near other materials of similar lengths.

4 Cut the hydrangea head into 1" sprigs of 3–4 individual blossoms each and glue evenly spaced
among the fern sprigs. Cut the larkspur into 3"–5" sprigs
and glue as for the fern. Use the ribbon to make a loopy
bow (see page 33) with four 1⅓" loops, two 1½" loops
and two 5" tails. Leave a 3" length of wire on the bow
and glue into the foam at the top edge of the holder rim.

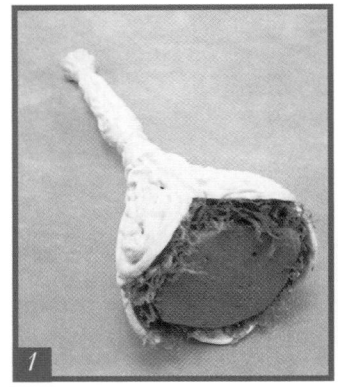

Heart-Shaped Box

one 9"x7½"x4" white rattan
    heart-shaped box with lid
6 stems of dark pink dried roses,
    each ¾" wide
2 oz. of green preserved
    plumosus fern
1 oz. of preserved lavender
1 oz. of pink dried ixodia daisies
1 oz. of dark plum preserved
    sinuata statice
1 yard of 1½" wide dark plum
    taffeta wire-edged ribbon
one 1" cube of floral foam for
    drieds
serrated knife
24-gauge wire
low temperature glue gun and
    sticks

1 Use the ribbon to make a standup bow (see page 33) with a 3½" loop, two 3" loops and two 7" tails. Glue it to the lid at the left, with the tails angling right. Use a knife to round the corners on the piece of foam. Glue it to the bow as shown.

2 Cut the plumosus into 3"–4" sprigs and glue into the foam, extending outward along the edges of the foam and upward in the center. Cut one rose to 3" and five to 2". Glue the 3" rose into the center of the foam, extending upward. Glue the remaining roses around it to form a triangle as shown.

3 Cut the lavender into 3"–5 sprigs and glue evenly spaced among the roses, extending as for the plumosus. Cut the ixodia daisies into 2"–3" sprigs and repeat.

4 Cut the statice into ½"–2" sprigs and glue evenly spaced among the other materials, extending outward around the outside and upward in the center.

Rustic Frames & Keepsake Box

For all the pieces:
4½ oz. of red dried pepperberries
4 oz. of dried papaver
4 oz. of dried birch branches
4 oz. of green sphagnum moss
3½ oz. of black/grey/white dried lichen
3 oz. of green mood moss
3 oz. of green shag moss
3 oz. of grey dried reindeer moss
2½ oz. of green dried linum
2¼ oz. of light green Spanish moss
2¼ oz. of light green dwarf's beard moss
acrylic paints: tan, moss green
wood sealer, paintbrush, sandpaper, clean cloth
24-gauge wire
low temperature glue gun and sticks

For the Mirror Frame:
one 14"x17" wood mirror frame

For the Picture Frame:
one 8"x6½" wood picture frame

For the Keepsake Box:
one 11"x4"x3" wood box with hinged lid
1 yard of 1" wide green wired woven paper ribbon

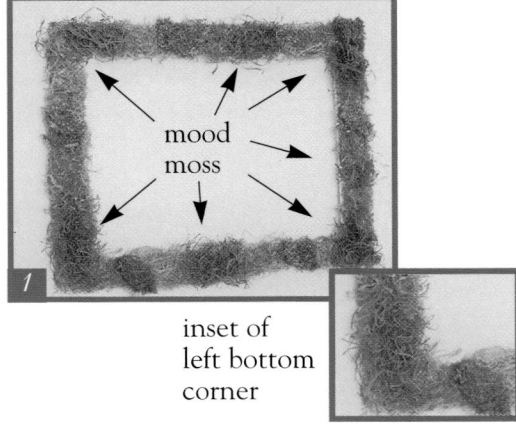

mood moss

inset of
left bottom
corner

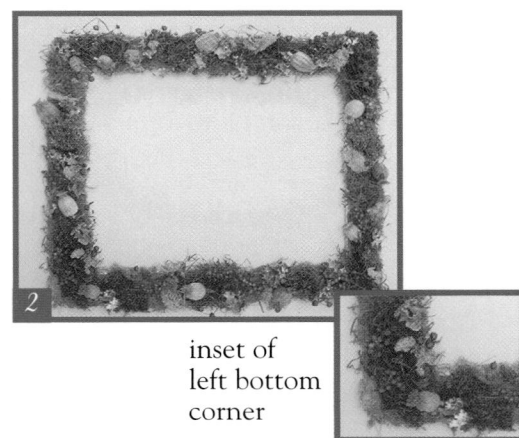

inset of
left bottom
corner

1 **For the Mirror Frame:**
Completely cover the frame front and sides with 2 oz. of sphagnum moss. Break 2 oz. of mood moss into 1½"–2" tufts and glue three tufts down the left side of the frame, two on the top, one on the right side and one on the bottom. Break 2 oz. of Spanish moss into 2" tufts and glue them evenly between the tufts of mood moss.

2 Break 2 oz. of lichen into ½"–2" tufts and 2 oz. of reindeer moss into 1"–2" tufts. Glue them evenly spaced among the mosses. Cut 2 oz. of papaver into 1" sprigs and glue evenly spaced to the frame, all extending clockwise. Cut 2 oz. of pepperberries into ½"–2" sprigs and glue evenly spaced among the moss. Cut 2 oz. of linum into 2"–3" sprigs and glue evenly spaced among the moss tufts with the sprigs on the sides and bottom extending upward and the top sprigs extending to the right.

3 Break 2 oz. of dwarf's beard and shag moss into 1"–3" sprigs and glue evenly spaced among the other materials. Cut 2 oz. of birch branches into 3"–7" twigs and glue among the mosses, with the sprigs on the sides extending upward and the sprigs on the top and bottom extending to the right.

4 **For the Photo Frame:** Sand the frame lightly, wipe clean, then paint the frame with the wood sealer; let dry. Paint it tan. While it is still wet, apply a small amount of green to the brush and lightly brush the frame for a streaked effect; let dry. Glue 1 oz. of sphagnum moss to the upper left corner of the frame as shown.

5 Cut six birch branches into eight 3"–5" twigs. Glue a few strands of dwarf's beard moss to each twig. Glue the twigs to the top left corner with three angling to the right and five angling downward. Tuck ¼ oz. of Spanish moss evenly among the twigs. Cut six small papaver stems into 2"–3" sprigs and glue among the twigs as shown. Cut ½ oz. of pepperberries into four 1" sprigs and glue among the papaver as shown.

6 Cut six 1" tufts of lichen and glue evenly spaced among the papaver and pepperberries. Cut six 1"–2" linum sprigs and glue evenly spaced among the other materials, with three sprigs on the left frame angling downward and three on the top angling right.

7 **For the Keepsake Box:** Sand, clean, seal and paint the box as described for the frame in step 4. Glue the ribbon around the lid edge. Glue a 2"x4" tuft of sphagnum moss to the lid center. Cut one 5" and two 4" sprigs of papaver and wire together near the cut ends. Glue to the lid, extending right. Repeat for the left side. Cut one 1" and four 2" sprigs of papaver. Glue the 1" sprig in the center of the moss, extending upward, and the others around it. Cover the stems with the remaining sphagnum moss.

8 Cut the remaining reindeer moss into 1"–2" tufts. Glue evenly spaced among the papaver sprigs. Cut the mood moss into eight ½"x1" sprigs. Glue four around the center papaver sprig, extending over the stems of the four 2" sprigs, and one on each side of the outer papaver sprigs.

 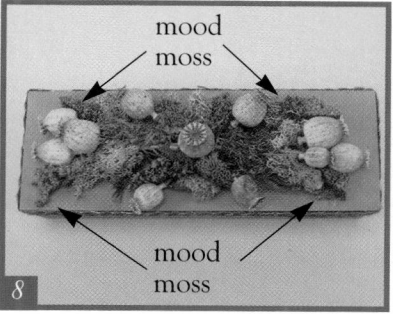

mood moss

mood moss

9 Cut the pepperberries into 1"–2" sprigs and glue evenly spaced among the other materials. Break the lichen into ½"–2" sprigs and glue among the mosses. Break the shag moss into 1" long tufts and glue evenly around the outside edge of the design, extending outward. Glue a few sprigs evenly spaced throughout the center.

10 Cut the birch branches into 3"–5" twigs and glue half on each side of the center papaver sprig, extending toward the ends. Use the center papaver sprig as a handle to open the box.

DECK THE HALLS

A festive wreath on the door and boughs of greenery tucked in nooks around the house say "Christmas is coming!" Creating special holiday decorations allows the ability to tailor them to fit a particular color scheme, style, and certain spaces. The designs on the following pages can become timeless complements to any decor and can easily be coordinated to work together by choosing similar flowers to use in several designs.

Several varieties of preserved evergreen boughs are available in rich shades of green and, in many cases, still hold their luxurious scent. Pine cones, mosses, bare twigs and seed pods, together with richly colored blossoms, berries and ribbons, can create impressive effects, whether they're designed in the traditional Christmas colors or in elegant, muted tones. With the available array of specialty floral paints and glitters, dazzling effects can also be achieved, highlighting the holiday decor.

Within this section are designs to match many decor styles. The Potted Wreath (page 132) and the Woodland Arrangement (page 133) both utilize deep shades of traditional colors for a look that is complementary to a natural, woodland setting or to country decor. For the traditionalist, we've included the Card Basket (page 142) and the Holiday Stocking (page 138), two beautiful designs featuring red, green and white.

The Christmas Star (page 141) adds shine and sparkle to a holiday and is an alternative to the traditional wreath. The Gilded Snow Garland (page 136) is elegant with white and multiple shades of green accented with gold on the leaves, cones and ribbon.

With the broad variety of styles in this collection of designs, creating decorative elements to grace any home for the holidays is not only fun, but simple too!

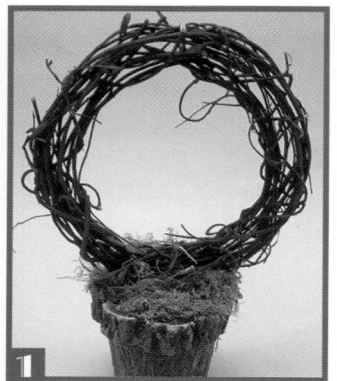

one 4½"x4½" bark flowerpot
one 9" round grapevine wreath
seven 2" long pine cones
six 5"–7" long pheasant feathers
4 oz. of green preserved cedar
2 oz. of red preserved bracken fern
2 oz. of preserved baby's breath
2 oz. of burgundy dried strawflowers
2 oz. of green sphagnum moss
1⅜ yards of 1½" wide green/burgundy/tan plaid wire-edged ribbon
4"x4"x4" block of floral foam for silks
6 U-shaped floral pins, 22-gauge wire, low temperature glue gun and sticks

1 Insert the foam into the container. Use U-pins to attach the wreath to the top of the foam, standing upright; add glue where the wreath touches the foam for reinforcement. Cover the foam with moss.

2 Cut the cedar into 2"–3" sprigs. Beginning at the bottom of the wreath, glue half the sprigs up each side, completely covering the wreath. Cut the fern into 3"–6" sprigs and glue them extending from the center bottom as shown.

3 Use the ribbon to make an oblong bow (see page 32) with a center loop, four 2½" loops, two 3" loops and 5" tails; trim each tail in an inverted "V." Glue the bow to the moss and wreath. Cut the baby's breath into 3"–5" sprigs and glue them evenly spaced among the fern sprigs.

4 Glue three pine cones evenly spaced among the florals on each side of the bow. Glue the last cone extending downward from the right center of the bow. Cut the strawflowers into 2"–4" sprigs and glue them evenly spaced among the fern and cones. Glue three feathers in a fan on each side of the bow, placing the longest feathers in the center positions and shorter ones above and below.

Woodland Arrangement

one 8"x4" round bark planter
11 stems of red dried roses, ¾"–1¼" wide
three 2"–3" wide dried lotus pods
4 oz. of green preserved boxwood
4 oz. of dried birch twigs
2 oz. of white dried larkspur
3 oz. of green preserved running cedar
3 oz. of green preserved austral fern
3 oz. of dried caspia
2 oz. of green sphagnum moss
one 6" block of floral foam for drieds
low temperature glue gun and sticks

1 Glue the foam into the center of the pot. Save a few tufts of moss for step 2; tuck the rest loosely around the foam. Cut the boxwood into 6"–13" sprigs. Insert 4–5 shorter sprigs into the right side, extending slightly outward. Insert the rest into the left side, with taller sprigs in the center and shorter ones angled to the outside.

2 Cut the birch twigs to 8"–15" long and insert them into the foam center with longer sprigs at the center back. Cut the fern into 6"–14" sprigs and insert them among twigs of similar lengths. Cut the roses to 5"–12" long and insert them into the center and right side with the longest in back, descending in length as you work forward. Insert the lotus pods in a triangle at the left and glue the remaining moss around them.

3 Cut the larkspur into 4"–12" sprigs and insert them into the center, right and left sides of the arrangement as for the roses. Cut the cedar into 4"–8" sprigs and insert them evenly spaced throughout the front half.

4 Cut the caspia into 4"–15" sprigs. Glue 4" sprigs around the lotus pods and along the lower front of the arrangement, extending outward and forward. Insert the rest evenly spaced throughout the design for fullness.

Cinnamon & Terra Cotta

terra cotta pots: one 1½", eight 2" wide
fifteen 16"–18" long dried cinnamon
   sticks
seven 1"–2" long pine cones
seven ¾"–2" wide orange strawflowers
one 2" wide green dried orange
4 oz. of green preserved running cedar
3 oz. of green preserved oak leaves
2 oz. of preserved baby's breath
1¾ yards of 2¾" wide green organza
   wire-edged ribbon
two ⅞" wide green plastic candle cups
22-gauge wire
low temperature glue gun and sticks

1 **For each candleholder:** Glue two 2" pots together bottom to bottom; repeat. Glue the two sets together rim to rim. Glue a candle cup into the top pot. **For the cinnamon bundle:** Wire the cinnamon sticks together at the centers.

2 Cut two 16" lengths of ribbon and use each to make a standup bow (see page 33) with a 3" loop, one 3" tail and one 4" tail. Glue one diagonally to the top joint of each candleholder, with the tails on opposite sides. Tie the remaining ribbon around the center of the cinnamon, making a shoestring bow (see page 35) with 3½" loops and 5" tails. Cut the cedar into 2"–6" sprigs. Glue three 2"–3" sprigs to the center of each standup bow. Glue the rest to the sticks, extending from the bow toward the ends.

3 Cut two 2" oak leaf sprigs and glue one to the bow center on each candlestick. Cut the rest of the oak leaves into 3"–6" sprigs and glue them among the cedar sprigs on the cinnamon bundle, angled as for the cedar. Glue the orange to the center of the shoestring bow.

4 Glue a 1" cone and a ¾" strawflower to each candleholder above the oak leaves. Glue the 1½" pot to the cinnamon bundle just right of the orange, angled right. Glue the remaining cones and strawflowers evenly spaced among the oak leaves on the bundle. Cut six 1" sprigs of baby's breath; glue three around the cone on each candleholder. Cut the rest of the baby's breath into 2"–3" sprigs. Glue three sprigs into the pot on the bundle and

the rest evenly spaced among all the cones and strawflowers.

Pods & Bay Leaves

one 30"x6" twig arch base

three 2" wide rope balls

three 2½" wide dried protea flats

two 1½" wide dried laranja pods

four 1½"–2½" long dried brazilia pods

three 2"–2½" wide dried sulphurea buds

6 oz. of green preserved oak leaves

4 oz. of green dried bay leaves or salal

2 oz. of dried achillea

3 oz. of brown dried pencil cattails

2 oz. of green dried festuca grass

2¼ yards of 1½" wide moss green satin ribbon

1¼ yards of 1¼" wide pale green organza wire-edged ribbon

two ⅞" wide green plastic candle cups

22-gauge wire, low temperature glue gun and sticks

1 Turn the arch so the ends point upward and attach a wire hanger (see page 26) to the back of each end. Cut the bay and oak leaves into 4"–6" sprigs. Working from each end toward the center, glue the sprigs to the arch extending toward the ends, alternating between oak and bay. Angle the sprigs as shown.

2 Glue a protea flat to the center of the arch and one 4" away on each side. Glue the laranja pods between the protea flats. Glue a sulphurea bud above the right protea, one below the center protea and one below the left laranja pod.

3 Glue a brazilia pod 2" above and right of the center protea. Glue another 2" below and left of the center protea. Glue the third 2" above the left protea flat and the last below the right laranja pod. Glue a rope ball 6" from each end of the arch and and one 1" above and left of the center protea.

4 Cut the achillea into 3" sprigs and the festuca and cattails into 4" sprigs. Glue them throughout the design, following the angles of the bay and oak leaves. Cut the organza ribbon in half and use each length to make a puffy bow (see page 32) with a center loop, two 2" loops and 5" tails. Cut the satin ribbon in half and use each length to make a puffy bow with four 3" loops and 7" tails. Wire an organza bow to the center of each satin bow. Glue one to each end of the arch.

Gilded Snow Garland

one 68" length of 4" wide white wire mesh ribbon
5½ yards of 1½" wide white/gold/green plaid wire-edged ribbon
five 3"–4" long gilded white pine cones
2 oz. of white glittered dried twigs
4 oz. of green preserved cedar
4 oz. of gold-glittered white preserved holly
3 oz. of gold preserved baby's breath
2 oz. of green preserved tree fern
2 oz. of gold dried salal or bay leaves
2 oz. of green preserved Fraser fir
22-gauge wire, low temperature glue gun and sticks

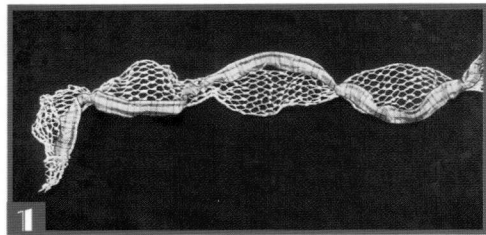

1 Bend 8" downward at a right angle on one end of the mesh ribbon and wire the bend, crimping it as you do so. Crimp and wire every 9" across the mesh, (a total of five times) bending the other end downward again. Cut a 70" length of plaid ribbon and drape it loosely across the mesh, wiring to secure it at each crimp. Attach a wire hanger (see page 26) behind the center and one behind each end.

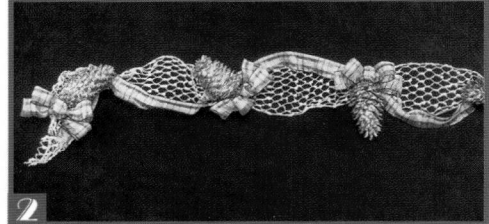

2 Cut the remaining ribbon into five 25" lengths and use each to make an oblong bow (see page 32) with a center loop, two 2½" loops, two 3" loops and no tails. Glue one in the center of each mesh tail and one to each of the three center crimps. Glue a pine cone to each bow, starting at the left and angling them as follows: first up and right; second up and left; third straight down; fourth left; fifth right.

3 Cut the twigs into 4"–8" sprigs and glue three to each tail, extending downward. Glue the rest across the garland, all extending right. Cut the cedar into 4"-8" sprigs. Glue 3–5 around each pine cone, angling a few downward along the tails. Use more sprigs for a fuller effect around the center cone. Cut the holly into 3"–6" sprigs and glue as for the cedar.

4 Cut the baby's breath and fern into 4"–6" sprigs and glue as for the cedar. Glue 2–3 salal leaves around each pine cone, angling the end leaves outward. Cut the fir into 3"–5" sprigs. Glue two around each of the outer four cones. Glue the rest evenly spaced on each side of the center cone, angled toward the ends.

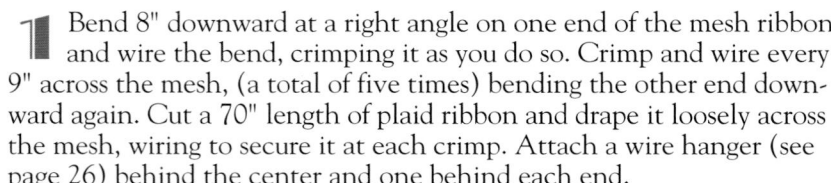

Majestic Metallics Wreath

one 18" wide green PVC
   pine wreath
five 3" wide matte-finish
   gold ball ornaments
three 3"–3¾" wide silver
   dried lotus pods
thirteen 1½"–2" long pine
   cones
3 oz. of gold dried wheat
3 oz. of green preserved
   salal or bay leaves

2 oz. of dried avena
2 oz. of dried nigella orientalis
2⅞ yards of 1½" wide mesh ribbon with copper satin stripes
spray paint for florals: silver, copper
22-gauge wire, low temperature glue gun and sticks

1 Attach a wire hanger (see page 26) to the top back of the wreath. Gather the wheat and pull up a few heads in the back. Wire it together under the heads. Glue the wheat to the wreath at 1:00 with the heads angled down toward 7:00. Use the ribbon to make a puffy bow (see page 32) with a center loop, six 3½" loops and one 55" tail. Glue the bow over the wired area of the wheat and weave the tail gently among the pine sprigs around the wreath.

2 Glue a gold ball at 3:00 and one at 10:00, centered on the wreath front. Glue others at 4:00, 8:00 and 12:00, placing these toward the outside of the wreath. Glue a lotus pod at 3:00 and one at 11:00, angled toward the inside edge of the wreath, and one at at 7:00, angled downward.

3 Mist the salal leaves with copper paint, gilding them lightly with green still visible. Spray the avena with copper as well, coating it heavily for an opaque finish. Let dry. Cut the avena into 4" sprigs and glue them evenly spaced among the pine sprigs, angling some clockwise and some counterclockwise. Cut the salal into 4"–6" sprigs and glue as for the avena.

4 Spray the orientalis silver; let dry. Cut it into 3" sprigs and glue in clusters of three evenly spaced throughout the design, angling the clusters toward the inside or outside to fill in any sparse areas. Glue the pine cones evenly spaced among the other materials.

Holiday Stocking

one 15"x9" red Christmas stocking with white trim
   and a ribbon hanger
2 oz. of white polyester fiberfill
thirteen ½"–¾" long pine cones
4 oz. of green preserved running cedar
2 oz. of white dried German statice
3 oz. of red dried roses, ¼"–½" wide
2 oz. of royal blue preserved peppergrass
1 oz. of green Spanish moss
1¼ yards of 2½" wide ivory/red/black plaid ribbon
22-gauge wire, low temperature glue gun and sticks

1 Stuff the stocking with fiberfill, leaving 3" empty at the top. Glue the foam on top of the fiberfill; glue the sides of the stocking to the foam. Cut two 9" cedar sprigs and insert one into each side of the foam, curving downward. Cut the rest of the cedar into 3"–6" sprigs. Glue them evenly spaced into the foam, angled upward.

2 Break the Spanish moss into 1"–2" tufts and insert them among the cedar sprigs to hide the foam. Use the ribbon to make an oblong bow (see page 32) with a center loop, two 2½" loops, two 3" loops, and 12" tails. Glue it to the upper left edge of the stocking; arrange and glue the tails as shown.

3 Cut the statice into 4"–6" sprigs and insert them into the foam evenly spaced among the cedar sprigs, at similar angles. Glue a few sprigs among the bow loops. Cut the roses into 4"–6" sprigs and insert them as for the statice.

4 Glue three pine cones around the center loop of the bow and the rest evenly spaced among the cedar and statice sprigs. Cut the peppergrass into 2"–4" sprigs. Glue four sprigs around the center bow loop and the rest evenly spaced among the cedar and statice.

Country Christmas Tree

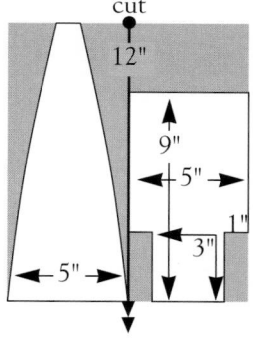

one 10"x12"x1½" sheet of Styrofoam®
nine 2" long pine cones
6 oz. of green preserved cedar
2 oz. of white dried German statice
1 oz. of raffia
2 oz. of 4" long cinnamon sticks
2 oz. of red dried pepperberries
2 oz. of green preserved tree fern
10 U-shaped floral pins
1⅛ yards of 2½" wide tan/burgundy gingham wire-edged ribbon
green spray paint for Styrofoam®
22-gauge wire, low temperature glue gun and sticks

1 **Tree base:** Cut the foam in half lengthwise and follow the diagram to trim away the gray areas. Glue the two sections together, matching the 5" ends; use U-pins to reinforce the seam. Make a U-pin hanger (see page 26) at the top back. Spray the front and sides green. Cut the cedar into 3"–6" sprigs and insert them into the foam, starting with the sides to establish a shape, then filling in the center. Angle the sprigs slightly outward and downward. Leave the trunk bare.

2 Cut an 8" ribbon length and wrap it around the trunk. Cut a 20" length and make a puffy bow (see page 32) with a center loop, two 2" loops and 3" tails; trim each tail in an inverted "V." Glue the bow over the trunk. Cut the remaining ribbon into one 3" and five 2" lengths. Cut the 2" lengths in half lengthwise and notch one end of each. Wire the other end tightly. Glue evenly spaced among the cedar sprigs. Notch both ends of the 3" length, wire it at the center and glue it to the tree top.

3 Cut the statice into 2"–3" sprigs and glue them evenly spaced among the cedar sprigs. Use the raffia to tie the cinnamon sticks together in bundles of three. Glue the cinnamon bundles among the cedar sprigs as shown, varying the angles.

4 Cut the pepperberries into 1"–3" sprigs and the fern into 2"–4" sprigs. Glue them evenly spaced throughout the design. Glue the pine cones evenly spaced throughout the design.

Gilded Holiday Wreath

one 22" round green PVC pine
 wreath
five 2"–3" wide dried pomegranates
five 2" wide brown dried cedar
 roses
eight 2"–3" long gold-tipped white
 pine cones
4 oz. of green preserved oak leaves
4 oz. of burgundy preserved holly
2 oz. of gray preserved stirlingia
2 oz. of bronze preserved salal
 leaves
2 oz. of white dried button flowers
2 oz. of gold dried caspia
2 oz. of white preserved rice flowers
2 oz. of green preserved misty
 limonium
1 oz. of gray dried lichen
22-gauge wire
low temperature glue gun and
 sticks

1 Attach a wire hanger (see page 26) to the top back of the wreath. Cut the holly and oak leaves into 4" sprigs. Glue them evenly spaced around the wreath, angled counterclockwise, angling toward the inner and outer edges. Break the lichen into three 3" tufts and glue one at 2:00, one at 6:00 and one at 10:00. Cut the stirlingia into 4" sprigs and glue them evenly spaced among the oak and holly leaves.

2 Glue pomegranates at 12:00, 2:00, 4:00, 7:00 and 9:00. Glue a cedar rose 1" below the 12:00 pome-granate. Glue another cedar rose at 3:00, one at 5:00, one to the upper right of the 7:00 pomegranate and one at 10:00.

3 Cut the salal leaves off the stems and glue them evenly spaced throughout the design, varying the angles. Glue the pine cones evenly spaced among the cedar roses and pomegranates. Cut the button flowers into 5" sprigs, divide into five equal clusters and glue them evenly spaced around the wreath.

4 Cut the caspia and the rice flowers into 4" sprigs and glue them evenly spaced throughout the design. Cut the misty limonium into 4"–6" sprigs and glue them angled counterclockwise among the other florals to fill in any open spaces, particularly around the inner and outer edges.

Christmas Star

one 18" wide lacquered twig star
one 2" wide white freeze-dried
    rose
seven 1"–1½" wide
    burgundy dried dahlia blos-
    soms
4 oz. of green preserved cedar
3 oz. of white dried ti tree
2 oz. of gold dried twigs
2 oz. of gold dried barley
2 oz. of white dried ixodia daisies
2½ yards of 3" wide burgundy
    organza ribbon with gold wired
    edges
2 yards of 1½" wide red/gold
    plaid wire-edged ribbon
22-gauge wire
low temperature glue gun and
    sticks

1 Attach a wire hanger (see page 26) to the star back at the base of the top point. Use the 3" ribbon to make a puffy bow (see page 32) with five 5" loops and 19" tails. Glue it at an angle to the upper left shoulder of the star. Ripple each tail diagonally across the front and glue near the bottom as shown. Cut the cedar into 5"–9" sprigs and glue them diagonally across the star, angled downward; glue a few shorter sprigs into the bow center and around the bow, angled as for the loops.

2 Use the plaid ribbon to make an oblong bow (see page 32) with a center loop, four 2½" loops, two 3½" loops and 18" tails. Glue it just under the puffy bow. Glue the dahlia blossoms evenly spaced among the cedar sprigs, with one above the bow.

3 Cut the ti tree into 4"–5" sprigs and glue them among the cedar sprigs with those below the bow angled downward and those around the bows angled as for the loops. Cut the gold twigs into 4"–6" sprigs and glue them as for the ti tree.

4 Glue the rose below the plaid bow center. Cut the barley into 4"–5" sprigs and glue them throughout the design, angled and spaced as for the gold twigs. Cut the daisies into 3"–5" sprigs and glue them evenly spaced among the previous materials.

Card Basket

one 11" round brown willow basket with an 8" tall handle
4 oz. of green preserved cedar
4 oz. of green preserved Fraser fir
3 oz. of gold dried barley
3 oz. of gray dried caspia
4 oz. of red dried roses with many ¼"–½" wide heads on each stem
1⅝ yards of 1" wide cream/gold wire-edged ribbon
22-gauge wire
low temperature glue gun and sticks

1 Cut the fir into 4"–7" sprigs and glue them to the left side of the basket, with some long sprigs extending up the handle and some across to the center front rim. Glue the shorter sprigs to the point where the handle meets the rim, angled outward, forward and toward the back. Cut the cedar into 3"–7" sprigs and glue them evenly spaced among fir sprigs of similar lengths and angles.

2 Use the ribbon to make a puffy bow (see page 32) with a center loop, six 2½" loops and 11" tails. Glue it to the left base of the basket handle and weave one tail upward among the evergreen sprigs. Weave the other one forward among the sprigs on the rim. Spot glue in several places to secure.

3 Cut the barley into 3"–5" sprigs and glue them throughout the design, angled and spaced as for the evergreen sprigs. Cut the caspia into 3"–5" sprigs and glue them evenly spaced among the other sprigs, angled in the same directions.

4 Cut the roses into 3"–6" sprigs. Glue several sprigs in a line extending from the base of the bow forward below the tail. Glue another line of sprigs above the bow, extending upward along the right side of the tail. Glue the rest of the sprigs evenly spaced among the other materials as shown.

Candleholder Centerpiece

one 12" straw wreath
one 5" wide blue/yellow dried hydrangea blossom head
twelve ½"–1" wide pine cones
four ⅞" wide green plastic candle cups
4 oz. of green preserved running cedar
2 oz. of green preserved boxwood
2 oz. of pink dried strawflower blossoms
2 oz. of red dried pepperberries
3 oz. of white dried ti tree
2 oz. of green sphagnum moss
2 oz. of preserved green reindeer moss
U-shaped floral pins, low temperature glue gun and sticks

1 Lay the wreath flat and cover with sphagnum moss, securing with U-pins. Glue the candle cups evenly spaced around the wreath. Cut the cedar into 2"–3" sprigs and glue it into the moss, evenly spaced around the wreath, with the outer sprigs angled downward.

2 Break the reindeer moss into 1"–2" tufts and glue them among the cedar sprigs evenly spaced around the wreath. Cut the boxwood into 3"–4" sprigs and glue them among the moss and cedar, angling the outer and inner sprigs downward.

3 Cut the hydrangea into 2"–3" sprigs and glue them around the wreath, alternating from inside to outside edge. Glue the strawflower blossoms throughout the design individually and in pairs as shown.

4 Cut the pepperberries into 2"–3" sprigs and glue evenly spaced around the wreath, angling the sprigs to extend over the inner and outer edges. Cut the ti tree into 2"–3" sprigs and glue throughout the design as for the cedar. Glue the pine cones evenly spaced, alternating from inside to outside around the wreath.

INDEX

BOOK ONE GROWTH RECORD

To measure growth, subtract pre-test score from unit test score; enter difference in the growth column.
(Note: Section test scores show progress along the way, but are not used in computing growth.)

UNIT I

Category	Pre-test	Section 1	Section 2	Section 3	Unit 1	Growth
A. Canon	%	%	xxxx	xxxx	%	%
B. Literature	%	xxxx	%	xxxx	%	%
C. History	%	xxxx	xxxx	%	%	%
Total	%	xxxx	xxxx	xxxx	%	%

UNIT 2

Category	Pre-test	Section 1	Section 2	Section 3	Section 4	Unit 2	Growth
A. Structure	%	%	%	%	%	%	%
B. Narrative	%	%	%	%	%	%	%
C. Features	%	xxxx	xxxx	xxxx	xxxx	%	%
Total	%	%	%	%	%	%	%

UNIT 3

Category	Pre-test	Section 1	Section 2	Section 3	Unit 3	Growth
A. Structure	%	%	%	%	%	%
B. Narrative	%	xxxx	%	%	%	%
C. Features	%	%	%	%	%	%
Total	%	%	%	%	%	%

UNIT 3 *(continued)*

Section Test 3

Category	# Correct		% Score	Directions
A. Structure	_____	=	_____	# correct x 20
B. Narrative	_____	=	_____	# correct x 10
C. Features	_____	=	_____	# correct x 10
Total (A+B+C)	_____ x4=		_____ %	

Unit Test 3

Category	# Correct		% Score	Directions
A. Structure	_____	=	_____	# correct x 10
B. Narrative	_____	=	_____	See % chart for 15.
C. Features	_____	=	_____	# correct x 4
Total(A+B+C)	_____ x2=		_____ %	

% CHARTS FOR SCORING

```
6   #   1   2   3   4   5   6#
    %  17  33  50  67  83 100%

8   #   1   2   3   4   5   6   7   8#
    %  13  25  37  50  63  75  87 100%

12  #   1   2   3   4   5   6   7   8   9  10  11  12#
    %   9  17  25  34  42  50  59  67  75  84  92 100%

14  #   1   2   3   4   5   6   7   8   9  10  11  12  13  14#
    %   7  14  21  28  36  43  50  57  64  72  79  86  93 100%

15  #   1   2   3   4   5   6   7   8   9  10  11  12  13  14   15#
    %   7  13  20  27  33  40  47  53  60  67  73  80  87  93  100%

18  #   1   2   3   4   5   6   7   8   9  10  11  12  13  14  15
    %   6  11  17  22  28  33  39  44  50  56  61  67  72  78  83

    #16  17  18#
    %89  94 100%
```

```
23 #  1   2   3   4   5   6   7   8   9  10  11  12  13  14  15  16#
   %  4   9  13  17  22  26  31  35  39  43  48  52  56  61  65  69%

   #17  18  19  20  21  22   23#
   %74  78  82  87  91  96  100%

30 #  1   2   3   4   5   6   7   8   9  10  11  12  13  14  15#
   %  3   7  10  13  17  20  23  27  30  33  37  40  43  47  50

   #16  17  18  19  20  21  22  23  24  25  26  27  28  29   30#
   %53  57  60  63  67  70  73  77  80  83  87  90  93  97  100%

35 #  1   2   3   4   5   6   7   8   9  10  11  12  13  14  15  16#
   %  3   6   9  11  14  17  20  23  26  29  31  34  37  40  43  46

   #17  18  19  20  21  22  23  24  25  26  27  28  29  30  31  32#
   %49  51  54  57  60  63  66  69  71  74  77  80  83  86  89  91%

   #33  34   35#
   %94  97  100%
```